1970

This book may be kept

FOURTEEN DAYS

THE REFERENCE SHELF   VOLUME 42 NUMBER 4

REPRESENTATIVE AMERICAN SPEECHES: 1969-1970

EDITED BY LESTER THONSSEN

Professor of Speech
Metropolitan State College of Colorado at Denver

THE H. W. WILSON COMPANY
NEW YORK   1970

THE REFERENCE SHELF

The books in this series contain reprints of articles, excerpts from books, and addresses on current issues and social trends in the United States and other countries. There are six separately bound numbers in each volume, all of which are generally published in the same calendar year. One number is a collection of recent speeches; each of the others is devoted to a single subject and gives background information and discussion from various points of view, concluding with a comprehensive bibliography. Books in the series may be purchased individually or on subscription.

REPRESENTATIVE AMERICAN SPEECHES: 1969-1970

Copyright © 1970
By The H. W. Wilson Company

International Standard Book Number 0-8242-0412-3

Library of Congress Catalog Card Number (38-27962)

PRINTED IN THE UNITED STATES OF AMERICA

PREFACE

The decade of the sixties began with high hope and promise. But the hope soon turned to anxiety, and the promise to fear and doubt and despair. A succession of events —assassinations, civil disturbances, racial clashes, disillusionments, widespread social and political unrest—seized the land. By decade's end, the nation was divisively embittered, and the public spirit dangerously eroded. The national mood approached the apocalyptic.

Of great achievements of the intellect, we could properly boast. Scientific and technological advances confounded belief. Men set foot on the moon—a feat of such daring and skill that millions of awestruck viewers wondered whether their eyes were not playing tricks on them.

Hovering ominously over the sixties, however, was the specter of war—the continuing war in Vietnam which Richard H. Rovere called, for Americans, "the supreme event of the decade." It affected every private and public action, tested old loyalties, aggravated unhealed wounds and opened up new ones. All serious topics of conversation, oratory, and debate returned sooner or later to the conflict in Southeast Asia.

An excerpt from an oration delivered 125 years ago may cast incidental light on the nature of our present condition. On July 4, 1845, Charles Sumner, abolitionist and later United States senator from Massachusetts, delivered an address entitled "The True Grandeur of Nations." He touched upon some abiding themes.

The true greatness of nations is in those qualities which constitute the greatness of the individual. It is not to be found in extent of territory, nor in vastness of population, nor in wealth; not in fortifications, or armies, or navies; not in the phosphorescent glare of fields of battle; not in Golgothas, though covered by monuments

3

that kiss the clouds; for all these are the creatures and representatives of those qualities of our nature which are unlike anything in God's nature.

The true greatness of a nation cannot be in triumphs of the intellect alone. Literature and art may widen the sphere of its influence; they may adorn it; but they are in their nature but accessories. The true grandeur of humanity is in moral elevation, sustained, enlightened, and decorated by the intellect of man. The truest tokens of this grandeur in a state are the diffusion of the greatest happiness among the greatest number, and that passionless Godlike justice, which controls the relations of the state to other states, and to all the people who are committed to its charge.

But war crushes with bloody heel all justice, all happiness, all that is Godlike in man. "It is," says the eloquent Robert Hall, "the temporary repeal of all the principles of virtue." True, it cannot be disguised that there are passages in its dreary annals cheered by deeds of generosity and sacrifice. But the virtues which shed their charm over its horrors are all borrowed of peace; they are emanations of the spirit of love, which is so strong in the heart of man that it survives the rudest assaults. The flowers of gentleness, of kindliness, of fidelity, of humanity, which flourish in unregarded luxuriance in the rich meadows of peace, receive unwonted admiration when we discern them in war, like violets shedding their perfume on the perilous edges of the precipice beyond the smiling borders of civilization. God be praised for all the examples of magnanimous virtue which he has vouchsafed to mankind! God be praised that the Roman emperor, about to start on a distant expedition of war, encompassed by squadrons of cavalry and by golden eagles which moved in the winds, stooped from his saddle to listen to the prayer of the humble widow, demanding justice for the death of her son! God be praised that Sidney, on the field of battle, gave with dying hand the cup of cold water to the dying soldier! That single act of self-forgetful sacrifice has consecrated the fenny field of Zutphen, far, oh! far beyond its battle; it has consecrated thy name, gallant Sidney, beyond any feat of thy sword, beyond any triumph of thy pen. But there are hands outstretched elsewhere than on fields of blood, for so little as a cup of cold water; the world is full of opportunities for deeds of kindness. Let me not be told, then, of the virtues of war. Let not the acts of generosity and sacrifice, which have triumphed on its fields, be invoked in its defense. In the words of Oriental imagery, the poisonous tree, though watered by nectar, can produce only the fruit of death!

Today many Americans view our condition darkly. They feel that the national conscience and spirit have been blighted. But one can yet hope and believe that there is ground for tempered optimism. An editorial statement in the New York *Times* may sound the prudent note:

To George Orwell, looking back, the decade of the thirties, born in the euphoric certainty of a quick return to "normalcy," was "a scenic railway ending in a torture-chamber." The sixties, launched in effect with the high inaugural hopes of John F. Kennedy, have gone almost but not quite as sour. May the seventies, entered solemnly and with trepidation, confound the prophets as thoroughly.

With this edition, I retire from the editorship of REPRESENTATIVE AMERICAN SPEECHES. Since 1959 it has been my pleasure to select yearly some fifteen or eighteen addresses which seemed worthy of remembrance. The satisfaction of the position was richly enhanced by the cooperation and counsel of the staff of The H. W. Wilson Company, by professional colleagues, and by my wife and friends who patiently discussed the merits of speeches at times when they doubtless had more pressing duties. For all these favors, I express warm gratitude.

LESTER THONSSEN

Denver, Colorado
August 1970

CONTENTS

THE PATTERNS OF CHANGE

A FRESH LOOK AT AN OLD SPEECH

THE CONTINUING AGONY

THE PURSUIT OF PEACE [1]

Richard M. Nixon [2]

"One of the oldest and most persistent problems in a democracy," wrote August Heckscher in *The American Scholar* in 1966, "is the degree to which there can be popular control of foreign policy and popular participation in decisions affecting war and peace." Much of the anguish in the nation during the past few years stems from this political dilemma. It was not only anguish, but a divisiveness which reached dangerous proportions in the constitutional crisis of mid-1970 over the extent of presidential power in committing the nation to extensions of the undeclared war in Southeast Asia.

In the face of mounting criticism of America's role in the Vietnam conflict, President Nixon has turned periodically to the public address, or modified "fireside chat," to advise the people of the state of the war. As reinforcers of confidence in the cause, these addresses have had mixed effects. But, in form and intent, they contain features not unlike those of the addresses of Franklin D. Roosevelt during World War II, Dwight D. Eisenhower during the Korean war, and John F. Kennedy during the Cuban episode. In a move designed to give the opposition party an opportunity to make its views known, especially following major addresses to the nation by the President, the Columbia Broadcasting System has offered free time for at least four short programs each year. Selected opposition leaders will have the opportunity to use the time to "answer the President."

President Nixon's series of talks began soon after his inauguration. On May 14, 1969—about four months after taking office—he addressed the nation on Vietnam. The burden of his message was twofold: (a) To show what plans the Government had rejected and (b) to indicate what solution we were prepared to accept. "We have ruled out," he said, "attempts to impose a purely military solution on the battlefield" and "we have . . . ruled out either a one-sided withdrawal from Vietnam or the acceptance in Paris of

[1] Address delivered over national radio and television, November 3, 1969. Text from Department of State Publication 8502.

[2] For biographical note, see Appendix.

terms that would amount to a disguised American defeat." He indicated that we were ready to accept "any government in South Vietnam that results from the free choice of the South Vietnamese people themselves."

During the following months, limited troop replacements were announced. On September 18, 1969, the President addressed the United Nations General Assembly. He repeated the principle set forth in his televised speech of May 14:

> What the United States wants for South Vietnam is not the important thing. What North Vietnam wants for South Vietnam is not the important thing. What is important is what the people of South Vietnam want for South Vietnam.

Perhaps the most widely discussed speech of the year, the address of November 3, 1969, came after a considerable build-up of publicity and expectation. It was announced prior to the massive Vietnam Moratorium demonstrations of October 15, and was in effect billed as a coming address of major consequence.

At the core of the address was the idea of Vietnamization—a plan which calls for the gradual shifting of the burden of battle to the South Vietnamese forces.

> . . . We really only have two choices open to us if we want to end this war.
>
> I can order an immediate, precipitate withdrawal of all Americans from Vietnam without regard to the effects of that action.
>
> Or we can persist in our search for a just peace through a negotiated settlement if possible, or through continued implementation of our plan for Vietnamization if necessary—a plan of which we will withdraw all of our forces from Vietnam on a schedule in accordance with our program, as the South Vietnamese become strong enough to defend their own freedom.
>
> I have chosen the second course.

Many of the President's critics had hoped that he would announce a cease-fire and/or additional withdrawals of American forces. He did neither.

For support of his proposals, the President appealed to the so-called silent majority.

> The more support I can have from the American people, the sooner that pledge [to end the war] can be redeemed; for the more divided we are at home, the less likely the enemy is to negotiate at Paris.

Let us be united for peace. Let us also be united
against defeat. Because let us understand: North Vietnam
cannot defeat or humiliate the United States. Only Americans can do that.

The "heady aftermath" of the speech, as *Newsweek* put it,
followed promptly. There was the usual count of letters and telegrams favoring the statement. But the critics of the war were generally unmoved by the presidential statement. The protesters saw
little in it that recognized the depth and force of their objections
to the war. Seasoned observers expressed varying opinions. Joseph
Alsop called it a successful technical feat of political leadership.
James Reston feared it might further polarize and divide the nation. Walter Lippmann thought the President should not "treat a
negotiated withdrawal as if it were a precipitate withdrawal." Continued Lippmann: "I . . . believe that a straightforward negotiated
withdrawal, which admits the failure of a mission but not the defeat of an army, will have a cleansing and healing effect on our
divided country." David Halberstam said the speech "seemed to
come from a time past, produced by the same illusions which produced the war." (For an extended critique of the speech, see
Robert P. Newman, "Under the Veneer: Nixon's Vietnam Speech
of November 3, 1969" in the *Quarterly Journal of Speech*, 56:168-
178, April 1970.)

According to New York *Times* writer Robert B. Semple, Jr.,
the speech went through ten drafts, "all written by the President
himself." Reportedly, he spent more time on it "than on any single
document since his acceptance speech to the Republican National
Convention in 1968."

Good evening, my fellow Americans:

Tonight I want to talk to you on a subject of deep concern to all Americans and to many people in all parts of the
world—the war in Vietnam.

I believe that one of the reasons for the deep division
about Vietnam is that many Americans have lost confidence
in what their Government has told them about our policy.
The American people cannot and should not be asked to
support a policy which involves the overriding issues of war
and peace unless they know the truth about that policy.

Tonight, therefore, I would like to answer some of the
questions that I know are on the minds of many of you listening to me.

How and why did America get involved in Vietnam in the first place?

How has this Administration changed the policy of the previous Administration?

What has really happened in the negotiations in Paris and on the battlefront in Vietnam?

What choices do we have if we are to end the war?

What are the prospects for peace?

Let me begin by describing the situation I found when I was inaugurated on January 20.

The war had been going on for four years. Thirty-one thousand Americans had been killed in action.

The training program for the South Vietnamese was behind schedule.

Five hundred forty thousand Americans were in Vietnam with no plans to reduce the number.

No progress had been made at the negotiations in Paris and the United States had not put forth a comprehensive peace proposal.

The war was causing deep division at home and criticism from many of our friends as well as our enemies abroad.

In view of these circumstances there were some who urged I end the war at once by ordering the immediate withdrawal of all American forces.

From a political standpoint this would have been a popular and easy course to follow. After all, we became involved in the war while my predecessor was in office. I could blame the defeat which would be the result of my action on him and come out as the peacemaker. Some put it quite bluntly: This was the only way to avoid allowing Johnson's war to become Nixon's war.

But I had a greater obligation than to think only of the years of my Administration and the next election. I had to think of the effect of my decision on the next generation and on the future of peace and freedom in America and in the world.

Let us all understand that the question before us is not whether some Americans are for peace and some Americans are against peace. The question at issue is not whether Johnson's war becomes Nixon's war.

The great question is: How can we win America's peace?

Let us turn now to the fundamental issue. Why and how did the United States become involved in Vietnam in the first place?

Fifteen years ago North Vietnam, with the logistical support of Communist China and the Soviet Union launched a campaign to impose a Communist government on South Vietnam by instigating and supporting a revolution.

In response to the request of the government of South Vietnam, President Eisenhower sent economic aid and military equipment to assist the people of South Vietnam in their efforts to prevent a Communist take-over. Seven years ago, President Kennedy sent sixteen thousand military personnel to Vietnam as combat advisers. Four years ago, President Johnson sent American combat forces to South Vietnam.

Now, many believe that President Johnson's decision to send American combat forces to South Vietnam was wrong. And many others—I among them—have been strongly critical of the way the war has been conducted.

But the question facing us today is—now that we are in the war, what is the best way to end it?

In January I could only conclude that the precipitate withdrawal of American forces from Vietnam would be a disaster not only for South Vietnam but for the United States and for the cause of peace.

For the South Vietnamese, our precipitate withdrawal would inevitably allow the Communists to repeat the massacres which followed their take-over in the North fifteen years before.

They then murdered more than fifty thousand people and hundreds of thousands more died in slave labor camps.

We saw a prelude of what would happen in South Vietnam when the Communists entered the city of Hue last year.

During their brief rule, there was a bloody reign of terror in which three thousand civilians were clubbed, shot to death, and buried in mass graves.

With the sudden collapse of our support, these atrocities of Hue would become the nightmare of the entire nation—and particularly for the million and a half Catholic refugees who fled to South Vietnam when the Communists took over in the North.

For the United States, this first defeat in our nation's history would result in a collapse of confidence in American leadership, not only in Asia but throughout the world.

Three American Presidents have recognized the great stakes involved in Vietnam and understood what had to be done.

In 1963, President Kennedy, with his characteristic eloquence and clarity, said, "we want to see a stable government there carrying on the struggle to maintain its national independence. We believe strongly in that. We're not going to withdraw from that effort. In my opinion for us to withdraw from that effort would mean a collapse not only of South Vietnam, but Southeast Asia, so we're going to stay there."

President Eisenhower and President Johnson expressed the same conclusion during their terms of office.

For the future of peace, precipitate withdrawal would thus be a disaster of immense magnitude.

A nation cannot remain great if it betrays its allies and lets down its friends.

Our defeat and humiliation in South Vietnam would without question promote recklessness in the councils of those great powers who have not yet abandoned their goals of world conquest.

This would spark violence wherever our commitments help maintain peace—in the Middle East, in Berlin, eventually even in the Western Hemisphere.

Ultimately, this would cost more lives.

It would not bring peace but more war.

For these reasons, I rejected the recommendation that I should end the war by immediately withdrawing all our forces. I chose instead to change American policy on both the negotiating front and the battlefront.

In order to end a war fought on many fronts, I initiated a pursuit for peace on many fronts.

In a television speech on May 14, in a speech before the United Nations, and on a number of other occasions I set forth our peace proposals in great detail.

> We have offered the complete withdrawal of all outside forces within one year.
>
> We have proposed a cease-fire under international supervision.
>
> We have offered free elections under international supervision with the Communists participating in the organization and conduct of the elections as an organized political force. The Saigon government has pledged to accept the result of the elections.

We have not put forth our proposals on a take-it-or-leave-it basis. We have indicated that we are willing to discuss the proposals that have been put forth by the other side. We have declared that anything is negotiable except the right of the people of South Vietnam to determine their own future. At the Paris peace conference, Ambassador Lodge has demonstrated our flexibility and good faith in forty public meetings.

Hanoi has refused even to discuss our proposals. They demand our unconditional acceptance of their terms, which are that we withdraw all American forces immediately and unconditionally and that we overthrow the government of South Vietnam as we leave.

We have not limited our peace initiatives to public forums and public statements. I recognized, in January, that a long and bitter war like this usually cannot be settled in a public forum. That is why in addition to the public statements and negotiations I have explored every possible private avenue that might lead to a settlement.

Tonight I am taking the unprecedented step of disclosing to you some of our other initiatives for peace—initiatives we undertook privately and secretly because we thought that we thereby might open a door which publicly would be closed.

I did not wait for my inauguration to begin my quest for peace.

Soon after my election through an individual who is directly in contact on a personal basis with the leaders of North Vietnam I made two private offers for a rapid, comprehensive settlement. Hanoi's replies called in effect for our surrender before negotiations.

Since the Soviet Union furnishes most of the military equipment for North Vietnam, Secretary of State Rogers, my Assistant for National Security Affairs, Dr. Kissinger, Ambassador Lodge, and I, personally, have met on a number of occasions with representatives of the Soviet government to enlist their assistance in getting meaningful negotiations started. In addition we have had extended discussions directed toward that same end with representatives of other governments which have diplomatic relations with North Vietnam. None of these initiatives have to date produced results.

In mid-July, I became convinced that it was necessary to make a major move to break the deadlock in Paris talks. I spoke directly in this office, where I am now sitting, with an individual who had known Ho Chi Minh on a personal basis for twenty-five years. Through him I sent a letter to Ho Chi Minh.

I did this outside of the usual diplomatic channels with the hope that with the necessity of making statements for propaganda removed, there might be constructive progress toward bringing the war to an end. Let me read from that letter:

Dear Mr. President:

I realize that it is difficult to communicate meaningfully across the gulf of four years of war. But precisely because of this gulf, I wanted to take this opportunity to reaffirm in all solemnity my desire to work for a just peace. I deeply believe that the war in Vietnam has gone on too long and delay in bringing it to an end can benefit no one—least of all the people of Vietnam. . . .

The time has come to move forward at the conference table toward an early resolution of this tragic war. You will find us forthcoming and open-minded in a common effort to bring the blessing of peace to the brave people of Vietnam. Let history record that at this critical juncture, both sides turned their face toward peace rather than toward conflict and war.

I received Ho Chi Minh's reply on August 30, three days before his death. It simply reiterated the public position North Vietnam had taken in the Paris talks and flatly rejected my initiative.

The full text of both letters is being released to the press.

In addition to the public meetings I referred to, Ambassador Lodge has met with Vietnam's chief negotiator in Paris in eleven private meetings.

We have taken other significant initiatives which must remain secret to keep open some channels of communication which may still prove to be productive.

But the effect of all the public, private and secret negotiations which have been undertaken since the bombing halt a year ago and since this Administration came into office on January 20, can be summed up in one sentence—

No progress whatever has been made except agreement on the shape of the bargaining table. Now who is at fault?

It has become clear that the obstacle in negotiating an end to the war is not the President of the United States. And it is not the South Vietnamese.

The obstacle is the other side's absolute refusal to show the least willingness to join us in seeking a just peace. It will not do so while it is convinced that all it has to do is to wait for our next concession, and the next until it gets everything it wants.

There can now be no longer any question that progress in negotiation depends only on Hanoi's deciding to negotiate, to negotiate seriously.

I realize that this report on our efforts on the diplomatic fronts is discouraging to the American people, but the American people are entitled to know the truth—the bad news as well as the good news, where the lives of our young men are involved.

Now let me turn, however, to a more encouraging report on another front.

At the time we launched our search for peace I recognized we might not succeed in bringing an end to the war through negotiation. I, therefore, put into effect another plan to bring peace—a plan which will bring the war to an end regardless of what happens on the negotiating front.

It is in line with a major shift in U.S. foreign policy which I described in my press conference at Guam on July 25. Let me briefly explain what has been described as the Nixon Doctrine—a policy which not only will help end the war in Vietnam, but which is an essential element of our program to prevent future Vietnams.

We Americans are a do-it-yourself people. We are an impatient people. Instead of teaching someone else to do a job, we like to do it ourselves. And this trait has been carried over into our foreign policy.

In Korea and again in Vietnam, the United States furnished most of the money, most of the arms, and most of the men to help the people of those countries defend their freedom against the Communist aggression.

Before any American troops were committed to Vietnam, a leader of another Asian country expressed this opinion to me when I was traveling in Asia as a private citizen. He said, "When you are trying to assist another nation defend its freedom, U.S. policy should be to help them fight the war but not to fight the war for them."

Well, in accordance with this wise counsel, I laid down in Guam three principles as guidelines for future American policy toward Asia:

First, the United States will keep all of its treaty commitments.

Second, we shall provide a shield if a nuclear power threatens the freedom of a nation allied with us or of a nation whose survival we consider vital to our security.

Third, in cases involving other types of aggression, we shall furnish military and economic assistance when requested in accordance with our treaty commitments. But we shall look to the nation directly threatened to assume the primary responsibility of providing the manpower for its defense.

After I announced this policy, I found that the leaders of the Philippines, Thailand, Vietnam, South Korea, and other nations which might be threatened by Communist aggression, welcomed this new direction in American foreign policy.

The defense of freedom is everybody's business—not just America's business. And it is particularly the responsibility of the people whose freedom is threatened. In the previous Administration, we Americanized the war in Vietnam. In this Administration, we are Vietnamizing the search for peace.

The policy of the previous Administration not only resulted in our assuming the primary responsibility for fighting the war but even more significantly did not adequately stress the goal of strengthening the South Vietnamese so that they could defend themselves when we left.

The Vietnamization Plan was launched following Secretary Laird's visit to Vietnam in March. Under the plan, I ordered first a substantial increase in the training and equipment of South Vietnamese forces.

In July, on my visit to Vietnam, I changed General Abrams' orders so that they were consistent with the objectives of our new policies. Under the new orders, the primary mission of our troops is to enable the South Vietnamese forces to assume the full responsibility for the security of South Vietnam.

Our air operations have been reduced by over 20 per cent.

And now we have begun to see the results of this long overdue change in American policy in Vietnam.

After five years of Americans going into Vietnam, we are finally bringing American men home. By December 15, over sixty thousand men will have been withdrawn from South Vietnam—including 20 per cent of all of our combat forces.

The South Vietnamese have continued to gain in strength. As a result they have been able to take over combat responsibilities from our American troops.

Two other significant developments have occurred since this Administration took office.

Enemy infiltration, infiltration which is essential if they are to launch a major attack, over the last three months is less than 20 per cent of what it was over the same period last year.

Most important—United States casualties have declined during the last two months to the lowest point in three years.

Let me now turn to our program for the future.

We have adopted a plan which we have worked out in cooperation with the South Vietnamese for the complete withdrawal of all U.S. combat ground forces, and their replacement by South Vietnamese forces on an orderly scheduled timetable. This withdrawal will be made from strength and not from weakness. As South Vietnamese forces become stronger, the rate of American withdrawal can become greater.

I have not and do not intend to announce the timetable for our program. There are obvious reasons for this decision which I am sure you will understand. As I have indicated on several occasions, the rate of withdrawal will depend on developments on three fronts.

One of these is the progress which can be or might be made in the Paris talks. An announcement of a fixed timetable for our withdrawal would completely remove any incentive for the enemy to negotiate an agreement.

They would simply wait until our forces had withdrawn and then move in.

The other two factors on which we will base our withdrawal decisions are the level of enemy activity and the progress of the training program of the South Vietnamese forces. I am glad to be able to report tonight progress on both of these fronts has been greater than we anticipated when we started the program in June for withdrawal. As a result, our timetable for withdrawal is more optimistic now than when we made our first estimates in June. This clearly demonstrates why it is not wise to be frozen in on a fixed timetable.

We must retain the flexibility to base each withdrawal decision on the situation as it is at that time rather than on estimates that are no longer valid.

Along with this optimistic estimate, I must—in all candor—leave one note of caution.

If the level of enemy activity significantly increases we might have to adjust our timetable accordingly.

However, I want the record to be completely clear on one point.

At the time of the bombing halt just a year ago, there was some confusion as to whether there was an understanding on the part of the enemy that if we stopped the bombing of North Vietnam they would stop the shelling of cities in South Vietnam. I want to be sure that there is no misunderstanding on the part of the enemy with regard to our withdrawal program.

We have noted the reduced level of infiltration, the reduction of our casualties, and are basing our withdrawal decisions partially on those factors.

If the level of infiltration or our casualties increase while we are trying to scale down the fighting, it will be the result of a conscious decision by the enemy.

Hanoi could make no greater mistake than to assume that an increase in violence will be to its advantage. If I conclude that increased enemy action jeopardizes our remaining forces in Vietnam, I shall not hesitate to take strong and effective measures to deal with that situation.

This is not a threat. This is a statement of policy which as Commander-in-Chief of our Armed Forces I am making in meeting my responsibility for the protection of American fighting men wherever they may be.

My fellow Americans, I am sure you recognize from what I have said that we really only have two choices open to us if we want to end this war.

I can order an immediate, precipitate withdrawal of all Americans from Vietnam without regard to the effects of that action.

Or we can persist in our search for a just peace through a negotiated settlement if possible, or through continued implementation of our plan for Vietnamization if necessary—a plan of which we will withdraw all of our forces from Vietnam on a schedule in accordance with our program, as the South Vietnamese become strong enough to defend their own freedom.

I have chosen the second course.
It is not the easy way.
It is the right way.
It is a plan which will end the war and serve the cause of peace—not just in Vietnam but in the Pacific and in the world.

In speaking of the consequences of a precipitate withdrawal, I mentioned that our allies would lose confidence in America.

Far more dangerous, we would lose confidence in ourselves. The immediate reaction would be a sense of relief that our men were coming home. But as we saw the consequences of what we had done, inevitable remorse and divisive recrimination would scar our spirit as a people.

We have faced other crises in our history and have become stronger by rejecting the easy way out and taking the right way in meeting our challenges. Our greatness as a nation has been our capacity to do what had to be done when we knew our course was right.

I recognize that some of my fellow citizens disagree with the plan for peace I have chosen. Honest and patriotic Americans have reached different conclusions as to how peace should be achieved.

In San Francisco a few weeks ago, I saw demonstrators carrying signs reading: "Lose in Vietnam, bring the boys home."

Well one of the strengths of our free society is that any American has a right to reach that conclusion and to advocate that point of view. But as President of the United States, I would be untrue to my oath of office if I allowed the policy of this nation to be dictated by the minority who hold that point of view and who try to impose it on the nation by mounting demonstrations in the street.

For almost two hundred years, the policy of this nation has been made under our Constitution by those leaders in the Congress and in the White House selected by all of the people. If a vocal minority, however fervent its cause, prevails over reason and the will of the majority this nation has no future as a free society.

And now I would like to address a word if I may to the young people of this nation who are particularly concerned, and I understand why they are concerned about this war.

I respect your idealism.

I share your concern for peace.

I want peace as much as you do.

There are powerful personal reasons I want to end this war. This week I will have to sign eighty-three letters to mothers, fathers, wives and loved ones of men who have given their lives for America in Vietnam. It is very little satisfaction to me that this is only one third as many letters as I signed the first week in office. There is nothing I want more than to see the day come when I do not have to write any of those letters.

I want to end the war to save the lives of those brave young men in Vietnam.

But I want to end it in a way which will increase the chance that their younger brothers and their sons will not have to fight in some future Vietnam someplace in the world.

And I want to end the war for another reason. I want to end it so that the energy and dedication of you, our young people, now too often directed into bitter hatred against those responsible for the war, can be turned to the great challenges of peace, a better life for all Americans, a better life for all people on this earth.

I have chosen a plan for peace. I believe it will succeed.

If it does not succeed, what the critics say now won't matter. Or, if it does succeed, what the critics say now won't matter. If it does not succeed, anything I say then won't matter.

I know it may not be fashionable to speak of patriotism or national destiny these days. But I feel it is appropriate to do so on this occasion.

Two hundred years ago this nation was weak and poor. But even then, America was the hope of millions in the world. Today we have become the strongest and richest nation in the world. The wheel of destiny has turned so that any hope the world has for the survival of peace and freedom will be determined by whether the American people have the moral stamina and the courage to meet the challenge of free world leadership.

Let historians not record that when America was the most powerful nation in the world we passed on the other side of the road and allowed the last hopes for peace and freedom of millions of people to be suffocated by the forces of totalitarianism.

And so tonight—to you, the great *silent majority* of my fellow Americans—I ask for your support.

I pledged in my campaign for the presidency to end the war in a way that we could win the peace. I have initiated a plan of action which will enable me to keep that pledge.

The more support I can have from the American people, the sooner that pledge can be redeemed; for the more divided we are at home, the less likely the enemy is to negotiate at Paris.

Let us be united for peace. Let us also be united against defeat. Because let us understand: *North Vietnam cannot defeat or humiliate the United States. Only Americans can do that.*

Fifty years ago, in this room and at this very desk, President Woodrow Wilson spoke words which caught the imagination of a war-weary world. He said, "This is the war to end wars." His dream for peace after World War I was shattered on the hard realities of great power politics and Woodrow Wilson died a broken man.

Tonight I do not tell you that the war in Vietnam is the war to end wars. But I do say this:

I have initiated a plan which will end this war in a way that will bring us closer to that great goal to which Woodrow Wilson and every American President in our history has been dedicated—the goal of a just and lasting peace.

As President I hold the responsibility for choosing the best path to that goal and then leading the nation along it.

I pledge to you tonight that I shall meet this responsibility with all of the strength and wisdom I can command in accordance with your hopes, mindful of your concerns, sustained by your prayers.

Thank you and good night.

WAR WITHOUT END [3]

FRANK CHURCH [4]

On April 30, 1970, in a nationally televised speech, President Nixon announced his decision to launch American and South Vietnamese attacks upon "major enemy sanctuaries on the Cambodian-Vietnam border." Thus began an operation which, according to an editorial in the *New Yorker* magazine, "precipitated one of the most dangerous crises in the nation's history." Protests over Vietnam and the extension of the war into Cambodia, and possibly into Laos, flared up with increased intensity and anger. Even moderates who had gone along, perhaps reluctantly, with the President's decisions in Southeast Asia were shaken by this new move. More and more the slogans seemed to say "It's time to leave." On May 27, 1970, *The Christian Science Monitor* urged editorially that the Administration "consider long and carefully before making any decisions or taking any steps which would appear to contradict the President's pledge to be out of Cambodia by June 30." In his speech of June 3, 1970, President Nixon declared the Cambodian action a success, said that all the Americans engaged in the operation would in fact be returned to Vietnam by June 30 and promised that the pledge of April 20 to send an additional 150,000 Americans home within a year would be kept.

Against the general background of the Vietnam war and the specific enlargement of it through the strike into Cambodia, Frank Church, senior senator from Idaho, spoke before the United States Senate on May 1, 1970, to reaffirm his vigorous objections to the conflict and to reflect on its apparent extension into other areas of Indochina. Mr. Church saw little reason for hope in the Vietnamization program:

> Novel as it may be, Vietnamization is a dangerous and unsound policy, more likely to lead to that "defeat and humiliation" which President Nixon so rightly deplores than to anything resembling an "honorable" peace. What it comes down to in plain common-sense terms is that, when you reduce your strength, you reduce your bargaining power. Thus far our withdrawals have not been sufficient to make a major difference in the military balance. But, by

[3] Speech delivered in the United States Senate, May 1, 1970. Text furnished by Senator Church, with permission for this reprint.

[4] For biographical note, see Appendix.

the spring of 1971, when American forces are scheduled to be reduced to around 265,000 men, the military balance will be significantly altered—unless the ARVN shows a far greater capacity of improving its effectiveness than we have any reason now to expect.

The only desirable way out of the crisis, Mr. Church declared, "is through a negotiated political settlement."

Subsequent to the delivery of this speech, Mr. Church, a Democrat, joined his fellow senator, John Sherman Cooper, Republican of Kentucky, in sponsoring the Cooper-Church Amendment which would prohibit the President from using any money for military activities in Cambodia without previous approval by Congress. Senator Majority Leader Mike Mansfield remarked in the Senate on June 22 that "Cooper-Church is not concerned with the constitutional powers of the presidency. Cooper-Church is an assertion of the constitutional responsibility of the Senate and Congress with regard to the war in Indochina and its evolving course." In late June, the Senate passed the Cooper-Church amendment to the Foreign Military Sales Act, but the House rejected it.

A highly accomplished speaker, Mr. Church was the keynote orator at the National Democratic Convention in 1960. During school and college days, he engaged actively in debate and other speaking competitions. In 1941 he was the national award winner of the American Legion Oratorical Contest. At Stanford University he won the Joffre Medal for distinction in debate.

When President Nixon took office fifteen months ago, he had two good choices and one bad one for dealing with the war in Vietnam. The promising choices were a negotiated peace based on a compromise coalition government in Saigon, coupled with the swift withdrawal of American forces; or, failing an agreement, a unilateral disengagement by the United States based on a phased but steady and complete withdrawal of American forces. In order to pursue either of these courses in those early days of his Administration when all options were open to him, the President would have had to acknowledge the futility of our continued military intervention in Vietnam. He would have had to admit—at least to himself—the impossibility of sustaining at any acceptable cost an anti-Communist regime in Saigon, allied with, dependent on, and supported by the United States.

This, of course, had long been the coveted objective of American policy in Indochina. Mr. Nixon was unprepared to abandon it. The result was the rejection of the two possible means of bringing the war to an early end and the adoption instead of the policy known as "Vietnamization." The tactics of the new course of action soon became clear: instead of escalating, we were going to deescalate, albeit by very gradual stages and over an indefinite period of time; instead of pouring in ever larger numbers of American troops, we were going to gradually substitute South Vietnamese forces in their place and thus keep the war going until the insurgents finally gave up their effort to displace the Saigon regime. Lost to view throughout the year 1969 was the fact that the new policy was only new in the means it employed; the objective remained unchanged.

We are still trying to maintain an anti-Communist regime, resistant to the North, in the southern half of a divided Vietnam. We are still determined to pursue an objective that makes necessary a permanent American military presence in Indochina. We are still bent upon preserving an American bridgehead on the mainland of Asia, next door to China. That is the meaning of Vietnamization.

In January 1969 Mr. Nixon inherited the leadership of an angry, divided and demoralized country. He had at that time a better opportunity than he will ever have to diagnose and treat the cause of the country's agony. In keeping with his own record and outlook, however, the new President did not perceive anything fundamentally wrong with the old policy. Instead, he saw only the symptoms: the high casualties, the inflated rhetoric, the student unrest, the Johnson "style" and the so-called "credibility gap."

It did not occur to Mr. Nixon that the policy itself was deeply unsound, extraneous to American interests and offensive to American values. The result was a change in tactics but not in goals. The policy has been repackaged; new, improved methods of salesmanship have been adopted; an optimistic new vocabulary has been introduced, full of bright promises of "peace with honor." Hopes have been buoyed by the return of part of our troops: people everywhere are saying that Vietnam is no longer an issue."

But the war goes on. American combat strength in South Vietnam has been reduced, but the war itself is spreading beyond the borders of Vietnam and has become an Indochina war. Nor is there any end in sight. The Administration has consistently refused to say—and perhaps does not even know—when if ever the American involvement will be brought to an end. Our withdrawal is said to be "irreversible," but the President continues to warn of "strong and effective measures" if the enemy takes military advantage of it. How a process of "irreversible withdrawal" can be reconciled with these "strong and effective measures" is not explained; nor is it explained what possible reason we might have for supposing that the enemy will not "take advantage" of our withdrawals.

The Nixon Administration has led us into a fundamental contradiction through its temporizing policy of scaled-down but indefinite warfare. The Johnson policy at least moved in one direction: an extravagant objective was matched by extravagant means. Mr. Nixon has moderated the means but retained the objective. The result is a masterpiece of incongruity, a design well conceived for futility and failure.

Sooner or later we are going to have to make a choice, matching our methods to our goals. If we continue to pursue the same extravagant objective in South Vietnam, the American military occupation of that country will have to be extended indefinitely. The alternative is to change the objective, to alter the policy. The latter, as I shall try once again to show, is the course of realism. Once we have chosen that course, once we have bitten the bullet of acknowledging past error, the means of extricating ourselves will pose no insuperable problems. Once we admit that this war is not now and never has been essential to American security, there should be no great difficulty about ending it. Until we do admit it, the war will go on.

It is no easy thing to admit an error but, as events have shown the scale and consequences of our mistaken venture in Vietnam, more and more Americans have been coming to the opinion that it is better to acknowledge a mistake than to perpetuate it. Even for those not directly involved, a good deal of maturity is required for facing up to a mistaken course of action. For statesmen and soldiers who have had personal involvement with the war in Vietnam, a high degree of fortitude and integrity is required. Nonetheless, an increasing number of men who fought this war have found it necessary to express their doubts about its justification. Late last year, for example, a former Air Cavalry captain who lost his right arm and both legs when he picked up a live grenade at Khe Sanh, summed up his own personal distress in these words:

To the devastating psychological effect of getting maimed, paralyzed, or in some way unable to reenter American life as you left it, is the added psychological weight that it may not have been worth it: that the war may have been a cruel hoax, an American tragedy that left a small minority of young American males holding the bag.

Distasteful though it is, we must review the reasons for our initial involvement in Vietnam. This is not just a case of confession being good for the soul. We need to understand the past so that we can act more wisely in the future. A clear comprehension of past mistakes is the only reliable insurance against repeating them. I do not agree, therefore, with President Nixon's assertion in his speech of May 14, 1969, that the "urgent question" is "not whether we should have entered on this course, but what is required of us today." The two, I believe, are connected: in order to determine "what is required of us today," it is indispensable that we understand why we did what we did in the past, and whether we should have done it.

If indeed the decision to intervene with an American army in 1965 was wise and sound, that would suggest that we now should continue the fight, with whatever force may be necessary, and for whatever time may be required. If, on the other hand, the intervention of 1965 was the result of faulty judgment, then it makes no sense to continue the war for a single day longer than is required to liquidate it in a decent and orderly way. There can be no cure without honest diagnosis. Yet, the Administration refuses even to think about past decisions in a critical or analytical way. Instead, it clings tenaciously and defensively to the discredited old arguments. The result is indecision and incongruity. As best I can make it out—and I do not think I can make it out with any real clarity—the Administration's position seems to be that the war is and always has been necessary and justified, but that political considerations rule out a greater military effort to win it, while they cannot bring themselves to end it either by a negotiated compromise or a phased but complete withdrawal.

The single most important source of this paralyzing ambiguity is the continuing prevalence of the myth of which Mr. Nixon himself was one of the principal perpetrators: the notion that communism is a single, unified, centrally directed, conspiratorial force unalterably committed to conquest of the world. Though often denied, the notion keeps turning up. Mr. Rusk used to warn of the danger of a "world cut in two by Asian communism." Mr. Nixon referred last November 3 to "those great powers who have not yet abandoned their goals of world conquest," and he predicted that American withdrawal from Vietnam would "spark violence wherever our commitments help maintain the peace—in the Middle East, in Berlin, eventually even in the Western Hemisphere." The President did not say how the "spark" would spread, but the explanation of why he thinks it would is implicit in his words: it is the old notion of the world Communist conspiracy, nurtured and sustained against all the compelling evidence which shows that, except in those areas such as Western Europe where the Russians bring direct physical power to bear, world communism has broken down into its national components, to such a degree that today communism is scarcely more united a force in the world than anticommunism.

In the case of Vietnam, it belabors the obvious—at least it would if the obvious were not under such steady challenge —to assert once again that the real force behind the long internal struggle is not ideology but Vietnamese nationalism. In his recent book on President Johnson's decision to end the escalation and initiate peace negotiations, Mr. Townsend Hoopes, the former Under Secretary of the Air Force, analyzed the war as follows:

North Vietnam was fighting *primarily* to achieve an unfulfilled national purpose. While it was, to be sure, fully aware of the implications for the wider application of the Mao-Ho-Giap insurgency doctrine, it was fighting not an abstractly ideological war, but a very particular war—in a particular place, characterized by a particular kind of terrain and weather, peopled by a particular breed of men and, above all, conditioned by a particular history. What really drove Ho's sacrificial legions was not the dream of world conquest, nor even the notion of generating a new momentum for Communist advance and triumph throughout Asia. What motivated Hanoi and enabled its leadership to hold nineteen million primitive people to endless struggle and sacrifice against odds that were statistically ludicrous was the goal of national independence.

If our minds were cleared of the Communist monolith obsession, we would perceive readily that the small country of North Vietnam, with which we have been at war for the last five years, is an authentically independent country, pursuing its own national objectives. These are the expulsion of foreign influence, the reunification of Vietnam and, quite probably, the establishment of their own dominant influence in all of former French Indochina. Though disagreeable to the United States and hardly benevolent, these designs are by no means to be confused with a conspiracy for the conquest of Asia. North Vietnamese ambitions are far less ideological, and much too restricted by the power limitations of a small, undeveloped country to be a serious threat to the United States, or even to those Southeast Asian countries which have any real measure of political coherence and support from their own populations.

Some Americans argue that we must stay in South Vietnam in order to prevent the population from falling under the yoke of a Communist dictatorship. Whatever altruism that idea may have in the abstract, it has little merit in actuality. For most of the people of Southeast Asia—certainly for the Vietnamese—there is no available democratic alternative. The choice lies between the harsh but relatively efficient and purposeful Communist dictatorship of North Vietnam and the equally harsh but corrupt and incompetent non-Communist dictatorship of South Vietnam.

Ideology in any case is of little consequence to poor and underdeveloped societies. Their requirements are more basic: they need governments which will refrain from robbing and plundering them, which will permit them the use and benefit of the land on which they live, and perhaps give them some assistance in cultivating it; which will provide basic medical services to protect them from common diseases; and which will provide at least elementary education for their children. Perhaps with time and development, political philosophy will acquire some importance for the villagers of Vietnam, Laos and Cambodia. In the meantime, nothing could be farther from their needs than those warring political ideologies which agitate the minds of statesmen in Washington, Moscow and Peking.

To suppose in any case that the regime which we are defending in South Vietnam has any knowledge of, interest in, or commitment to, democratic freedoms requires a greater capacity for self-delusion than is to be found among any but that dwindling band of old-school cold warriors whose demeaning definition of a democratic government is any regime, however decadent, which preaches undying hostility to communism.

Another superficially compelling rationalization for our continued participation in this war in which we have no vital interest of our own is the threat of a massacre in South

Vietnam if we should leave. Raising this specter in his
speech of November 3, Mr. Nixon warned that our "precipitate withdrawal would inevitably allow the Communists
to repeat the massacres which followed their take-over in the
North fifteen years before." Even if it were as certain as the
President takes it to be that a victorious Vietcong would
murder large numbers of South Vietnamese civilians, it is
not a rational policy to hold off this calamity by perpetuating
the killing of both Vietnamese and Americans in the war.
Even if the Communists were to do everything that Mr.
Nixon fears, it is doubtful that they could match the daily,
continuing bloodbath of the war itself.

For this has become a war of indiscriminate killing on
both sides. Unable to distinguish between soldiers and civilians, as likely to have a grenade thrown at him by a woman
or child as by an identifiable soldier, the American G.I. has
learned to shoot first and ask questions later. He is doing no
more than any of us would do under the circumstances—but
he *is* doing it.

This war in which the enemy is indistinguishable from
the people is the real bloodbath in Vietnam. To continue it
so as to prevent possible Communist reprisals after the war
is to rely on the same perverse logic as that contained in the
now famous words of the American major who said after the
Tet Offensive in 1968: "We had to destroy Ben Tre in order
to save it."

If once we made the decision that we were going to withdraw from Vietnam—finally and completely—it should be
possible to have guarantees for the lives of South Vietnamese
civilians included among the provisions of a negotiated settlement. The North Vietnamese—for what it is worth—insist
that they have no intention of perpetrating a peacetime massacre. They say that they are prepared to live and even co-
operate with anyone who favors the "independence, peace
and neutrality" of South Vietnam.

If in the end we should withdraw without a formal peace
settlement, it would be a matter of honor to provide asylum

for those South Vietnamese who might be unwilling to trust their fate to Communist promises. If it came to that, it would be far better to open our own gates to those who felt themselves endangered than to keep on sending Americans to die for them in their own land. As for the Saigon generals, there should be ample facilities for them on the French Riviera.

On all counts, the evidence is overwhelming that this war is not necessary, that, indeed, its continuation is immensely detrimental both to our own interests and to those of the peoples involved. We keep fighting in Vietnam because we are not yet willing to acknowledge that we should never have gone there in the first place. The result is a policy of pure contradiction: torn between its stubborn adherence to the war and its political need to get out of it, the Nixon Administration has devised a policy with no chance of winning the war, little chance of ending it, and every chance of perpetuating it into the indefinite future—the policy called "Vietnamization."

The official logic of Vietnamization is that, by some miraculous means, we are going to strengthen our bargaining hand by weakening our military effort. It is indeed a unique strategy, quite probably unprecedented in the history of warfare: bringing pressure to bear on the enemy by withdrawing from the battlefield. As the President explained it in his press conference of December 8, 1969, gradual American withdrawal is supposed to induce Hanoi to negotiate on our terms because, as he put it, "once we are out and the South Vietnamese are there, they will have a much harder individual to negotiate with. . . ." If the President was speaking of Mr. Thieu's attitude toward negotiations, there can be no argument: he is much "harder." But the President neglected to mention that it is not the *political* toughness of the South Vietnamese that is going to count if American forces are withdrawn but their *military* toughness, and in that department—despite the optimism expressed by the President in his speech of April 20—they are hardly a match for their

Communist adversaries. That, let it never be forgotten, is why we went there in the first place.

Novel as it may be, Vietnamization is a dangerous and unsound policy, more likely to lead to that "defeat and humiliation" which President Nixon so rightly deplores than to anything resembling an "honorable" peace. What it comes down to in plain common-sense terms is that, when you reduce your strength, you reduce your bargaining power. Thus far our withdrawals have not been sufficient to make a major difference in the military balance. But, by the spring of 1971, when American forces are scheduled to be reduced to around 265,000 men, the military balance will be significantly altered—unless the ARVN shows a far greater capacity for improving its effectiveness than we have any reason now to expect. What if the Communists then undertake a massive offensive aimed at winning the war outright? Would we then reescalate the war, taking those "strong and effective measures" of which President Nixon has repeatedly warned, or would we accept the defeat?

Neither American military personnel in Vietnam nor the South Vietnamese themselves are sanguine about the prospects of Vietnamization. According to staff members of the Senate Foreign Relations Committee who went on a study trip to Vietnam in December, 1969, American military officers have very little to say about the prospect for South Vietnamese military self-sufficiency, and when they do talk about it, it is in the time span of two to four years. President Thieu said recently that the withdrawal of American ground combat forces by the end of 1970 was an "impossible goal" and that, instead, "it will take many years" to remove these forces. President Nixon said nothing in his speech of April 20 to indicate a different assessment on his part.

Congress is as much in the dark as everybody else about the timetable for Vietnamization. Even in closed session of the Senate Foreign Relations Committee, the Secretaries of State and Defense have consistently declined to indicate how long the process is expected to take and how many Americans might remain in South Vietnam for the indefinite future. It is well to remember that there are still fifty thousand American soldiers in Korea, seventeen years after the end of the Korean War, despite the fact that the Republic of Korea has a large and effective army of its own, a defensible frontier, and freedom from internal subversion. How many Americans may be required to sustain the Saigon regime, which has none of the assets of South Korea? The Administration steadfastly refuses to divulge the answer—if indeed it has one.

Even if it worked, Vietnamization would be a futile policy, because it no longer covers the situation in Southeast Asia. "I feel," the late Vietnam expert Bernard Fall once remarked, "like it is 1913, and I am an expert on Serbia who is about to be outstripped by events." The import of Fall's apprehension was that Vietnam might one day be consumed in a far wider conflict just as the Serbian controversy was consumed and then forgotten in the flames of World War I. One hopes it will never come to that, but the spread of hostilities to Laos and Cambodia has already made it obsolete to speak of a "Vietnamese" war. In fact, with or without official recognition, we are now quite busily engaged in what Fall had the prescience several years ago to perceive as a "second Indochina war," a sequel to the struggle between the Vietminh and the French for domination of the entire Indochinese peninsula.

Increasingly the North Vietnamese and even the Chinese are referring to the conflicts in Vietnam, Laos and Cambodia as a single "struggle for Indochina." As Mr. Stanley Karnow, one of the most perceptive journalists reporting from Indochina, commented recently: ". . . the Communists are making it clear that they are prepared to expand the war over the artificial boundaries that separate the Indochinese states, and there is no reason to doubt their intentions."

There is hope as well as menace in this new situation, depending upon how the Nixon Administration responds to it. If it follows the counsel of some of its military and civilian advisers in Vietnam and expands American military activities in Laos and Cambodia, then a predictable spiral of challenge and response will soon put an end both to Vietnamization and deescalation of the war. If, on the other hand, Mr. Nixon and his advisers see what Bernard Fall perceived long ago, that there can be no solution to Vietnam except in the context of a general solution to Indochina, they might then revise their entire strategy and put us for the first time on a sensible course toward peace.

Stalemated by superior American firepower in Vietnam, the Communists appear to have embarked upon a general Indochinese strategy aimed at surrounding and isolating the American position in South Vietnam.

In Laos, despite a momentary abatement of hostilities, the military strength of the American-supported army of Meo tribesmen appears to be slowly deteriorating. Although the Communists have made no thrust toward the administrative capital of Vientiane, their dominance over northeastern Laos is virtually unchallenged except by continuing American air attacks. These air strikes, according to reports, are being conducted round the clock, amounting to an estimated eighteen thousand sorties a month. Meanwhile, despite fearful harassment from the air, the North Vietnamese continue to move supplies across the Plain of Jars toward the few remaining anti-Communist strongholds in northeastern Laos.

As an American diplomat recently explained to a diligent reporter:

The important thing is that the clandestine army is being destroyed and the U.S. bombing cannot stop it. This happens every day, in little skirmishes you never hear about. When Long Tieng finally crumbles, the Communists will have consolidated their hold on northeast Laos. American bombing can make life hell for them, but it cannot stop them. Laos, in its typically leisurely way, is going down the drain.

In truth, our position in Laos borders on helplessness. Secretary of State Rogers all but confessed as much in a television statement on March 17. "We hope," he said, "that what they are up to is to make their negotiating position a little stronger. We hope that they do not intend to overrun Laos."

Whatever the precise Communist objective in Laos, it is already having the effect of undermining the foundations of the Nixon Vietnamization policy. In a military sense, it raises the long-term prospect of locking American forces into a beleaguered South Vietnamese enclave, while North Vietnam establishes its hegemony over the rest of Indochina.

Aside from continuing our indecisive bombing campaign in Laos and hoping for the best, the Administration has two equally distasteful alternatives. It can simply give up any further hope of salvaging Laos and thereby see its Vietnamization strategy undermined by indirection; or it can send American ground forces, or a greatly increased number of Thais, into the Laotian war, thereby abandoning the Vietnamization strategy and reverting to escalation. In the latter event, there is no telling where the escalation would stop. In a phrase reminiscent of the days before their "volunteers" swarmed into Korea in 1950, the Chinese have already responded to the entry of Thai forces into Laos with the warning that they "will not sit idly by."

The situation is hardly more promising in Cambodia; it may indeed be worse. With more bravado than wisdom, the new regime of General Lon Nol has undertaken to drive the North Vietnamese and Vietcong forces out of the borderlands of Cambodia. The trouble is that the weak little Cambodian army is in no position to do it without massive American help, and that, in fact, is exactly what appears to be in the offing.

With indeterminate but unmistakable American support, South Vietnamese troops have been striking at North Vietnamese and Vietcong units inside Cambodia. The Communists in turn have called on the Cambodian people to overthrow their new government and are using their forces within Cambodia to weaken the new regime. The Pnompenh regime, for its part, is showing itself impotent against the Vietcong, while its troops, with or without official approval, have committed atrocious mass murders of Vietnamese civilians living in Cambodia.

It has long been the desire of American and South Vietnamese military officials to attack the Communist sanctuaries in Cambodia. From a purely military standpoint this is understandable, but the political implications are ominous. They raise the possibility of escalation in still another direction, under circumstances the Thieu government must surely welcome as a golden opportunity to put an end to American troop withdrawals by plunging the United States into a wider, Indochinese war.

Mr. Nixon and his advisers may feel tempted to come to the support of the anti-Communist but powerless new regime in Pnompenh. On the other hand, the Administration must surely recognize the risks involved in an expansion of the war into Cambodia. The Vietcong and North Vietnamese have already turned that formerly neutral country into a battleground, and done so with the blessing of the ousted Prince Sihanouk, who has cloaked the Communists with legitimacy by creating a government in exile and by calling for a "National Liberation Army" to fight "with other anti-imperialist peoples forces of fraternal countries."

It escapes my understanding how, under these altered circumstances, the Administration still fails to recognize that it is involving itself in an Indochina war which can only be resolved by an Indochina strategy. To continue relying on Vietnamization under these circumstances is comparable, in Bernard Fall's World War I analogy, to throwing resources into Serbia long after the Western Front had exploded. The Communists have made it abundantly clear that they are not going to allow us to press our military advantage in Vietnam without circumventing it by exploiting the power vacuums in Laos and Cambodia. Even more to the point, they have made it abundantly clear that, although they cannot expel us from Indochina, they are able and determined to thwart the policy of Vietnamization. The premise of that policy is that American intervention can be reduced to a level at which it may be sustained indefinitely without undue political disruption at home. That premise has been discredited by events in Laos and Cambodia, if not indeed by conditions in Vietnam as well. We are going to have to plunge into Indochina all the way and face the enormous consequences at home and abroad, or we are going to have to get out.

The obvious and desirable way out is through a negotiated political settlement. President Nixon, however, appears to have given up on the Paris negotiations, insisting that the only alternative to Vietnamization is "immediate precipitate withdrawal." The North Vietnamese government, he told Congress in his report of February 18, "has adamantly refused even to discuss our proposals" and, further, "has insisted that we must unconditionally and totally accept its demands for unilateral U.S. withdrawal and for the removal of the leaders of the government of South Vietnam." He repeated this in scarcely altered words on April 20.

Reports by numerous unofficial and foreign observers suggest that the President's reading of the North Vietnamese position is inaccurate. Reputable individuals who have met with North Vietnamese officials both in Hanoi and in Paris assert that they do not insist on a complete American withdrawal prior to the conclusion of a settlement, nor do they demand a Vietcong take-over of South Vietnam. What they do insist upon, according to these observers, is an American commitment to a definite schedule for complete withdrawal of American forces and a transitional coalition regime to rule in Saigon until such time as a permanent government can be constituted. What the North Vietnamese and Vietcong are not able to accept are the following: an indefinite American military presence; the continuation of the present South Vietnamese constitution—known to them as the "Johnson constitution"—which prohibits Communists from any participation in the government; and control of the election procedure for a permanent government by the present Saigon regime.

Aside from the continued presence of American forces in Indochina, the crucial question is quite simply: who is going to rule South Vietnam? The only feasible basis for compromising that question is a sharing of power between the warring factions; the appropriate term, so much out of favor, is a "coalition." When all the political manifestos and diplomatic terms of art are set aside, the conditions for peace in South Vietnam are clear: either some form of coalition is going to be formed, or the war is going to go on until one side or the other prevails.

If we can agree to these two basic conditions—ultimate, total American withdrawal by a definite date and some form of coalition—a negotiated peace is probably attainable. My own belief, for the reasons I have tried to spell out, is that a settlement along these lines is consistent with our interests, compatible with the security of Southeast Asia, and quite possibly in the best interests of the South Vietnamese people. It is obviously not a desirable arrangement from the personal standpoint of Mr. Thieu and Mr. Ky, but—lest it be forgotten—we are not as a nation committed to those two gentlemen or to their political careers.

The real question on which the prospect for a negotiated peace turns is the attitude of President Nixon and his advisers. If they can bring themselves to acknowledge the character of America's interests in Southeast Asia, the realities of an Indochina war and the necessity for an Indochina settlement, the logjam might be broken more speedily than anyone now supposes. If, on the other hand—and as seems more probable—they cling to the crumbling premises of Vietnamization, there can be little prospect of a negotiated settlement. In that event, it would seem appropriate for the Congress, with its own special responsibilities for foreign policy, to reevaluate its position and the resources available for giving weight to its judgments.

In the belief that Congress has the responsibility—not just the right but the responsibility—to provide the President with advice as well as consent in matters of foreign policy, a number of us in the Senate have taken legislative initiatives in recent months designed to advance the kind of peace settlement which we believe to be in our national interest. Most of these legislative proposals have been hortatory rather than mandatory, designed to encourage the President as strongly as possible to bring the war to an early end but not to impose upon him an inflexible course of action.

The Administration has scarcely shown any interest, much less responsiveness, to the various recommendations of Senators of both parties—except in those few instances in which Senators have praised or endorsed the course which the Administration is already following. It has, therefore, seemed appropriate to go a step beyond exhortation and to begin to use the explicit war and appropriations powers vested in the Congress by the Constitution.

To this end, I joined with the majority leader, Senator Mansfield, and my distinguished Republican colleague on the Senate Foreign Relations Committee, Senator Cooper, in sponsoring last December an amendment to the fiscal 1970 military appropriations bill prohibiting the use of any funds under that bill "to finance the introduction of American ground troops into Laos or Thailand." The Church-Cooper amendment was adopted by a four-to-one-margin—73 to 17.

This week, Senator Cooper and I announced that we shall ask the Senate to expand this prohibition to include Cambodia, which has now been invaded by South Vietnamese troops aided and supported by American forces.

In addition, Senator Cooper and I are joined this week by Senator Mansfield and the ranking Republican member of the Foreign Relations Committee, Senator Aiken, in the sponsorship of an amendment to the pending military-sales bill that would, if adopted, prohibit the delivery of arms, or the introduction of American military instructors or advisers, into Cambodia, and set the limits on any American participation in combat within or above Cambodia.

It is unquestionably within the constitutional power of the Congress to bar the dispersal and delivery of American military weapons, services and supplies to a foreign government. Legislative prohibitions are needed now, because of the pending request of the new Cambodian government for military aid from the United States. No reliable assessment exists in respect to this new Cambodian government. We know not of its character; nor do we know the limits of the popular support it may command. Moreover, the United States owes no obligation to this new government; we have no defense treaty with it—nor with its predecessor. We have made no previous commitment to Cambodia. We have no responsibility to come to its defense. Yet, without giving Congress any prior notice, let alone asking for its consent, President Nixon has already started through the opened door. He has ordered American forces to participate with South Vietnamese in an invasion of Cambodian territory. This is done in the name of denying the enemy its supply depots and forward bases just within Cambodia's borders. But when it comes to sanctuaries, we would do well to remember that all of Asia behind the enemy line is its "sanctuary." We would do well to remember that we have our "sanctuaries" too—in Thailand, for example. If this is now to become a war in pursuit of "sanctuaries," then past experience suggests that each new thrust will be met with a counterthrust, and the war will spread.

Moreover, once the Cambodian boundary has been breached, it takes no exercise of the imagination to forecast that pressures will soon develop for sending a full-scale American military mission into that country which, in turn, will generate a whole new set of American obligations to defend the new Cambodian regime. It is this very sequence of events that led us ever deeper into the morass in Vietnam. We travel down that tragic trail again in Cambodia.

The overriding concern for us in Southeast Asia should be the military situation in South Vietnam, where our troops are already so heavily committed. Here, our position has not been altered by the recent overthrow of Sihanouk. For years now, the Vietcong and North Vietnamese have been utilizing border bases in Cambodia. But this Administration, like its predecessors, had accepted that very condition. President Nixon himself had premised his policy of "Vietnamization" on acceptance of that condition. By extending aid to South Vietnamese troops invading Cambodia, the President has opened up a new war front in Indochina and, thereby, has placed in the gravest jeopardy his declared policy of de-escalating American participation in the war.

The time has come for the Congress to draw the line against an expanded American involvement in this widening war.

Too much blood has been lost . . . too much patience gone unrewarded . . . while the war continues to poison our whole society. Whether by a negotiated compromise or by a phased, orderly but complete American withdrawal, it is time to put an end to it. If the Executive Branch will not take the initiative, then the Congress and the people must— the longer the bankrupt policy of Vietnamization continues, the closer it brings us to that which it purports to avoid: disaster and defeat.

THE IMPACT ON THE AMERICAN ECONOMY OF THE VIETNAMIZATION PROGRAM [5]

John T. Connor [6]

During late spring 1970, the Senate Foreign Relations Committee heard testimony on the impact of the war in Southeast Asia on the nation's economy. Included among the witnesses were Eliot Janeway, writer and business consultant; Louis B. Lundborg, chairman of the board, Bank of America; Gordon Sherman, president of Midas International Corporation; and Thomas J. Watson, Jr., chairman of the board, International Business Machines. All were in substantial agreement that the war had significantly induced an unhealthy state in the economy. In his remarks, Mr. Watson declared that there were two compelling reasons for his wanting a prompt end to the war: "First, I don't think we can afford not to heed the dissatisfaction of youth. Second, it seems certain to me that continuing the war produces unacceptable costs: in the lives of our fighting men, in weakening of our institutions, and in the undermining of our national morale."

A similar view was expressed in the speech reprinted here. On May 8, 1970, before a meeting of the Business Council in Hot Springs, Virginia, John T. Connor assessed the impact of the war, and especially the Vietnamization program, on the national economy. He concluded that the time to be silent had passed; the time had come to "speak out against the continuation and expansion of this senseless warfare." Mr. Connor, who is chairman of the board of Allied Chemical Corporation, was forthright in his remarks before this gathering of notable industrialists. It may very well not have been the kind of address his audience expected. But reportedly friends of Mr. Connor know that he is not given to the muting of convictions deeply and seriously held.

John Harper took quite a chance when he asked me to predict the impact on the American economy of President Nixon's Vietnamization program of bringing our troops home and turning over military responsibilities to the South

[5] Address delivered at the Business Council Meeting in Hot Springs, Virginia, May 8, 1970. Text furnished by Mr. Connor, with permission for this reprint.

[6] For biographical note, see Appendix.

Vietnamese. Certainly it's a topic on which we need as much information as we can get. Some industries and areas are already feeling the program's effects, and all of us should prepare for an intensification of the process in the months ahead. That is, of course, we should prepare for an intensification if in fact the Vietnamization program is still relevant. Our recent military actions in Cambodia raise serious doubts about the future of the program, and I question whether my discussion of its economic effects is worth your while. Putting aside the Cambodian complications for the moment, I will go ahead and make some assumptions and predictions about the Vietnamization program and its economic effects. In so doing, however, I want to remind you that my track record on predictions is not very impressive.

The embarrassing fact is that my past predictions about what would happen in Vietnam, or what would happen in the United States and elsewhere in the world because of Vietnam, have been rather wide of the mark. Many of you will recall that Sidney Weinberg and I, among others, were instrumental in persuading some of you to take a public stand in support of the Johnson-Humphrey ticket in 1964. Our most persuasive argument was that some of Senator Barry Goldwater's statements were alarming because they indicated that, if elected President, he would lead us into a ground war in Asia. Many of us were gravely concerned about the domestic and foreign consequences of that kind of escalation in Vietnam, and we decided to support President Lyndon B. Johnson on the ground that his actions and words clearly indicated that *he* wouldn't involve us in any Asian ground war. We know now that President Johnson maintained that position only until the 1964 election was firmly hung on the wall. The cheers of victory were still ringing when he authorized a sharp escalation of our troop commitments in Vietnam, although the facts of the escalation and its scope were kept secret from the American people and the Congress for some time. I don't have to spell out the tragic consequences of that decision, nor of President Johnson's subsequent decisions to escalate again and again, always said to be justified by the desire to end the war quickly and bring the boys home. Thousands and thousands of lives have been lost or ruined, our foreign relations have been jeopardized, serious social problems have been caused, our young people have become bitter, reckless and disillusioned, and disastrous inflation rages in the national economy, affecting all of us.

Without making any predictions, I shall assume that with a slight interruption we will soon be back on the track of deescalation in Vietnam, and that the President will again emphasize the Vietnamization program in the manner that won the confidence of so many of us in his speech last November 3d.

Making that hopeful assumption, I can proceed to discuss Vietnamization, first, in the general context of the social and economic environment of the day.

Then I want to indicate the economic impact of Vietnamization under three headings: (1) the aggregate impact; (2) the impact on specific industries; and (3) the impact on regions and communities.

Finally, I want to discuss some of the policy implications for business and government stemming from Vietnamization.

As for the general social and economic environment, I don't see how we can escape the conclusion that some kind of momentous reordering of priorities is taking place in our country.

We aren't sure of its meaning, or where it's leading us, but apparently its effects will be vast and far reaching. The many changes wrought by the social revolution of the 1930s come to mind as a comparison of what may be taking place today. Its manifestations include a sharpened aversion to war, a deep concern for the environment, a desire for equality of opportunity for all, and a general longing to do something about the urban and population crises. Perhaps the phrase we hear so much, "a new concern for the quality of American life," sums up about as well as anything else the great tidal wave of change in national mood and outlook that is taking place.

Our most sensitive barometer of changes in national aims is, of course, our political institutions. And President Nixon's Budget Message for fiscal year 1971 reflected the current change when he said, "For the first time in two full decades, the Federal Government will spend more money on human resource programs than on national defense."

I think we have all concluded, from the President on down, that we cannot win victories abroad on the foundation of defeats at home. Certainly we must maintain a defense establishment second to none in this dangerous age of nuclear weapons. But we must also demonstrate that our system can build a better life for our own people, if we hope to help lead the world in the ways of peaceful progress.

Now let's turn to the economic impact of the Vietnamization program.

Recognizing the many uncertainties, we'll assume that the disengagement can be accomplished on schedule. We do not know, however, how much or what kind of support the South Vietnamese army will require after our ground combat forces are withdrawn. We do not know the quantity of supplies they will need if the fighting continues, nor the number of supporting American troops that may remain.

In addition, any measurement of the impact of Vietnamization is complicated by the fact that some defense cuts have been made that may have little relation to the war in Southeast Asia. Some older and ineffective weapons systems are being retired, some bases are being closed, other military activities are being consolidated or reduced. While these cuts can often be separated from those resulting from Vietnamization, our national economy does not differentiate between their effects. Nor do we always segregate the substantial reductions being made in the space program, which uses many of the same resources as defense.

On the other hand, there are counterbalancing expenditures planned for new weapons systems for both our strategic

and general-purpose forces. The proposed 1971 budget provides for several such programs that had been deferred for
several years as the Vietnam outlays rose.

With these caveats in mind, let's zero in as best we can on
the impact of Vietnamization.

First, the aggregate impact.

As you probably know, the Defense Department has published no specific cost breakdown for the war, but fairly ac-
curate estimates can be arrived at.

In a new Brookings Institution study he cited in testify-
ing before the Senate Foreign Relations Committee last week,
former Budget Director Charles Schultze estimated that the
outlays for Vietnam were at an annual rate of $23 billion at
the end of fiscal 1969, almost a year ago. He expects the figure
to be about $17 billion by the end of the current fiscal year
next month. And in the fiscal year ending June 30, 1971, the
annual rate will be down to about $11 billion.

This figures out to a total cutback of about $12 billion for
Vietnam over a two-year period. But the cut in budget outlays for all national defense from fiscal 1969 to 1971 is not
that meaningful. The 1971 defense budget calls for outlays of
$73.6 billion, down $5.8 billion from 1970 and $7.6 billion
below 1969.

Another measurement of the possible aggregate impact of
Vietnamization can be seen in manpower figures.

The total involved is comprised of three categories: military personnel, civilian personnel in the Defense Department, and defense related employment in the private sector.
Sharp reductions are already scheduled for each of these
three categories.

The budgeted cut in military personnel is about 550,000
over the two-year period fiscal 1970-71. The troop withdrawals from Vietnam over this period equal about half this
number. Including the President's most recent announcement, these withdrawals will total about 265,000. That will
leave some 285,000 American troops in Vietnam a year from
now.

The cut in civilian personnel on the Defense Department payroll will amount to more than 130,000 in the two-year period. That brings the total Defense personnel reductions, including the military, to about 680,000 by June 30, 1971.

In addition, the Defense Department estimates that total program cuts in fiscal years 1970-71 will cause a dislocation of about 650,000 in contractor personnel. Half of these workers will have been let out by the end of next month, with most of the remaining cuts to take place by the end of June 1971.

The total of these reductions—in military and Defense Department civilian personnel, plus contractor personnel—will be more than 1.3 million, about 1.6 per cent of the total labor force.

In addition, we must include the workers engaged in producing the consumer goods and services required by contractor and Defense personnel. This calculation involves the multiplier effect of defense spending, which is felt directly in many localities by merchants, barbers and beauticians, as well as by manufacturers of consumer goods. A University of Michigan study has shown that each dollar of war outlay generates about 85 cents of additional output of consumer goods. So during this present adjustment, the producers of consumer goods and services, as well as defense contractors, are likely to feel the increasing effects of defense cutbacks, at least until the defense workers and servicemen find other employment.

As a recent Labor Department study pointed out, even a total withdrawal from Vietnam would not mean that 1.3 million jobs would be lost. Deferred non-Vietnam requirements will probably keep overall defense employment at a high level, and in some industries increased civilian demand would take up the slack. There is no question, however, that the movement of resources from defense to domestic uses, such as is now taking place, can cause adverse economic impacts. The Defense Department Comptroller, Mr. Robert Moot, pointed to this fact last month in comparing today's cutbacks with those after the Korean war.

Following the conclusion of hostilities in Korea, military spending, which reached its peak in 1953, dropped sharply in 1954. The reduction in defense purchases was $11 billion, or 15 per cent, and represented 3 per cent of the GNP (gross national product). It contributed significantly to the onset of a recession, during which unemployment increased from 2.9 per cent to 5.5 per cent and real GNP declined by 1.4 per cent.

In the Vietnam war period from 1969 to 1971 defense purchases are slated to be reduced by $7.6 billion in current dollars, or slightly in excess of 9 per cent. In relation to GNP, the decrease would be less than 1 per cent, suggesting a markedly smaller aggregate impact on the economy than in the post-Korean years. In constant dollars the cutback in military spending over the two-year period will be significantly greater, but not great enough to alter the conclusion with respect to its overall impact on the economy. The present mild contraction in general business activity and the recent rise in unemployment from 3.5 per cent to 4.4 per cent are mainly a result of the restrictive monetary and fiscal policies and the eroding effect of inflation on the purchasing power of consumers, with declining defense outlays being only a contributing factor. The economic effects can be more serious, of course, if all the adverse factors accumulate before there is the recovery and upswing in the national economy now predicted for the second half of 1970.

Now let's turn to some of the specific industries that will feel the impact of Vietnamization the most.

The Labor study is our best guide here. It pinpoints the industries most affected by the Vietnam build up and which presumably are most likely to be affected by withdrawal.

Aircraft, ordnance, and transportation are at the top of the list. Together they accounted for almost 40 per cent of the increase in defense employment due to Vietnam.

In aircraft, more than 230,000 jobs were in Vietnam-related production at the height in 1968. They accounted for 27 per cent of the industry's total employment.

In ordnance, the number was 140,000 jobs—42 per cent of the industry's total. Most were in ammunition production, which will be cut back severely. The study pointed out that increased missile expenditures will probably help to counter the overall decline in employment in the ordnance industry, but this would not affect ammunition workers.

In transportation, there were 165,000 Vietnam-related jobs, but this number represents only 6 per cent of the industry's total. Many were in Pacific shipping and airlines, and west coast warehousing.

Other industries with 10 per cent or more of their employment due to Vietnam were communications equipment, electronics, textiles, and machine shop products. Still further down the list were shipbuilding, 7 per cent; primary nonferrous metal manufacturing, 6 per cent; electrical equipment, 6 per cent; and scientific instruments, 5 per cent.

All these industries, and many of their suppliers, will feel the Vietnam cutbacks unless other military orders or demand from the civilian sector take their place.

Now let's consider the geographical impact of Vietnamization.

During the cold war period, the arms build-up was largely concentrated in highly sophisticated strategic weapons. These were manufactured largely in the southern and western areas of the country which were more suitable for testing the new weapons.

Vietnam required a shift to conventional weapons associated with limited warfare—ammunition, vehicles, textile and clothing products, and other supplies of an ordinary kind. The older manufacturing regions—the Midwest, the South Central and the New England regions—already had established suppliers of these needs, and therefore received relatively greater increases in defense orders during the Vietnam build-up.

While the cutbacks will be greatest there, these older regions also have relatively higher concentrations of production in civilian goods. They therefore will be able to absorb

the impact of the cutbacks better than the newer manufacturing areas along the Pacific coast and in the Mountain
states, which are more heavily dependent on defense expenditures.

But while a whole region or even a large metropolitan
area with a diversified economy can take such reductions
without too much difficulty, small communities cannot.
There, a shutdown of a manufacturing facility or closing of
a military base can result in serious local unemployment, de-
clines in retail sales and construction, and depressed property values. Older and low-skilled workers are particularly
vulnerable.

Beyond this summary of the cutbacks is what they mean
to the economy and what measures Government can take to
ease the adjustments during the demobilization period. Certainly we want to avoid a downturn similar to that following
the Korean war.

To that end our Government today is providing expanded manpower training for workers and increased educational assistance for veterans. For communities hit by cutbacks, other Federal resources are being channeled in, or
facilities in abandoned bases are being developed to attract
industry.

In the planning efforts of recent years, much attention
has been focused on how to maintain aggregate demand to
compensate for the reduction in defense expenditures.
Measures suggested included tax cuts, a speedup of Government spending on existing projects, a launching of new programs and easier monetary policies. But the current inflation
adds a new factor to the equation. In fact, the Vietnam cutbacks have been considered in some quarters as a welcome
assist to the fight on inflation. Our major preoccupation today is not the stimulation of the economy, but how to mod-
erate the strong forces that have been working for expansion.
At least, this was the view in March of Mr. Murray L. Wei-
denbaum, Assistant Secretary of the Treasury for Economic
Policy and a long-time student of the economic conse-

quences of a Vietnam pullout. He pointed out that Vietnamization would reduce the demand for military goods and services and, as servicemen are returned to civilian life, they would increase the labor force available to produce goods and services for nonmilitary purposes.

The Administration's policy has become somewhat less restrictive since March, but I think it's proper to characterize it still as one of "responsible restraint." The course that the Government officials must set for the future, however, is not easy to chart. The measures to be taken must be timely and appropriate if we are to avoid even more serious inflation than we now have, on the one hand, or a severe cumulative contraction, on the other.

Two weeks ago we could have said that there was little question but that the cloud of Vietnam was finally lifting. President Nixon's commendable program to disengage seemed to be working and to be more or less on course. His plans had the backing and support of a large majority of the American people and the members of Congress, and he had our confidence. It is true that his more recent commitment about bringing home troops was more long range in its timing, extending over a full year, rather than a more specific short-range commitment, but yet he seemed to indicate a firm resolve to continue on course.

Now we seem to have made a 180-degree change in direction. The President's decision to support the Vietnamese border crossing into Cambodia with American troops and other means set us off on a new course of action that shakes the confidence of many Americans in his judgment and intentions. In his speech justifying the decision the President attempts to reassure us by saying:

This is not an invasion of Cambodia. The areas in which these attacks will be launched are completely occupied and controlled by North Vietnamese forces.

Our purpose is not to occupy the areas. Once enemy forces are driven out of these sanctuaries and once their military supplies are destroyed we will withdraw.

These actions are in no way directed to security interests of any nation. Any government that chooses to use these actions as a pretext for harming relations with the United States will be doing so on its own responsibility and on its own initiative and we will draw the appropriate conclusions.

Despite those soothing words the troop movements into Cambodia, followed by the renewed aerial bombing of North Vietnam, shocked and stunned many of us because they certainly do amount to an escalation of the recent level of military activities. What happens from now on will depend to a great extent on the reactions of the North Vietnamese, the Chinese Communists and the Russians, and we already have the disquieting initial reactions from them. The earlier escalation moves directed by President Johnson invariably met with reactions from our enemies that finally resulted in an unsatisfactory military stalemate and caused intense and widespread human suffering, as well as a tremendous waste of assets that could have been used much more productively to satisfy human needs.

Certainly the Cambodian decision has precipitated a constitutional crisis of the most serious nature. The Congress is now moving to reassert its constitutional responsibilities to the American people and make it clear to the world that the President does not have unlimited power to wage war on his own initiative. Within the populace at large it is already clear that the Cambodian move will result in more widespread dissension in this country, involving many other loyal citizens besides most of the young, the intellectuals and the blacks. This time many of the silent majority will cease to be silent and will speak out against the continuation and expansion of this senseless warfare.

We hope that the President is right in his evaluation and that these new moves will in fact save lives and shorten the war. But we can't forget that too often in this war other escalating moves were made to achieve the same objectives. Their results were invariably disappointing, and we found ourselves bogged down time and time again in jungle warfare for which we are ill prepared and for which we have no heart. My personal view is that we should pull back and terminate these new offensive measures, and continue our disengagement program quickly, before it is too late. Any loss of face and any real or imagined blow to our national pride involved in a pullback weighs lightly in the balance against the dreadful consequences of further escalation into an all-out war in Southeast Asia and perhaps elsewhere.

Despite the immediate economic and other problems and dislocations, I think many of us can agree that for the long term a Vietnam disengagement would gain us many benefits of a social, humanitarian, economic and political nature in this country and around the world. Any continuation, much less an intensification, of the Vietnam war is bad for American business, every bit as much as it's harmful for the people of the United States generally.

There is every indication that in these final three decades of the twentieth century our technological revolution will accelerate even faster than it has in recent years. This will require enormous investments in new plants and equipment, in skilled manpower, more scientists, more engineers, more technicians and more experienced and skilled managers.

Certainly there will be no lack of demand. Our mush-rooming population may well reach 300 million by the year 2000. The markets for housing, pollution control, better transportation, education, health and recreational facilities will dwarf anything we've seen in the past.

We shall need all the resources we can get—human and material—to satisfy the demand. And then some! For the benefits of the long term, therefore, it is clear that we should put the immediate problem in proper perspective and con-tinue to support the Vietnamization program of disengage-ment and withdrawal. Only in that way can we have the opportunities to enable us to solve our nation's urgent problems.

THOUGHTS ON BROADCAST JOURNALISM

ADDRESS BEFORE THE MIDWEST REGIONAL REPUBLICAN COMMITTEE [1]

Spiro T. Agnew [2]

In an interview in late November 1969, Vice President Spiro T. Agnew disavowed any intention of launching a spiritual crusade. He was simply expressing thoughts, he observed, which "abraded some revered dogmas of the Fourth Estate." And abrade they did. His speechmaking has been persistent—some seventy addresses during his first nine months in office. The first major statement to release a flood of comment was the New Orleans speech of October 19, 1969, in which he commented on a "spirit of national masochism . . . encouraged by an effete corps of impudent snobs who characterize themselves as intellectuals."

In all likelihood, Mr. Agnew's most controversial address was in effect a follow-up to President Nixon's Vietnam statement of November 3, 1969. Immediately after the delivery of the presidential address, selected newsmen and commentators evaluated the talk. They had received advance copies of the text about two hours before it was given. Mr. Agnew did not find the tone and substance of this "instant rebuttal" wholly to his liking. So on November 13, 1969, in a televised address delivered before a regional meeting of the Midwest Regional Republican Committee in Des Moines, Iowa, the Vice President took to task the "little group of men who not only enjoy a right of instant rebuttal to every presidential address, but more importantly, wield a free hand in selecting, presenting and interpreting the great issues of our nation."

His concern over the networks and many commentators was essentially twofold: (a) He objected to the practices which, in his view, denied the people "the right to make up their own minds and form their own opinions about a presidential address without having the President's words and thoughts characterized through the prejudices of hostile critics before they can even be digested." (b) He sensed a danger in the power exercised by "a tiny and

[1] Address delivered before the Midwest Regional Republican Meeting in Des Moines, Iowa, November 13, 1969. Text furnished by Vice President Agnew, with permission for this reprint.

[2] For biographical note, see Appendix.

closed fraternity of privileged men, elected by no one, and enjoying a monopoly sanctioned and licensed by Government." Such
monopoly, he believed, was peculiarly objectionable because the
favored fraternity did not "represent the views of America."

The response to the Des Moines speech was instantaneous,
often acerbic, and to this day, unremitting. In the meantime, however, Mr. Agnew continued his speechmaking, addressing himself
to such topics as student unrest, protesters, open admissions, American journalism, vocational education, and the hierarchy of human values.

Mr. Agnew's speechmaking attracts wide public attention.
And few people are neutral toward it; they either like it or they
don't. Through *words,* perhaps more than through official position,
he has become a household name. His rhetoric—a heavily used
term these days—is the subject of a continuing debate. In fact, a
delegation of eleven University of Minnesota professors met with
the Vice President in early June and urged him "to tone down his
rhetoric," lest it help drive the "moderates into the arms of extremists." According to a report in the New York *Times,* a vice
presidential aide quoted Mr. Agnew as saying the discussion "was
certainly of value to me."

Students of political oratory may wish to read Martin Mayer's
"The Brilliance of Spiro Agnew" in the May 1970 issue of *Esquire*
magazine.

Tonight I want to discuss the importance of the television news medium to the American people. No nation depends more on the intelligent judgment of its citizens. No
medium has a more profound influence over public opinion.
Nowhere in our system are there fewer checks on vast power.
So, nowhere should there be more conscientious responsibility exercised than by the news media. The question is . . . are
we demanding enough of our television news presentations?
. . . And, are the men of this medium demanding enough of
themselves?

Monday night, a week ago, President Nixon delivered
the most important address of his Administration, one of
the most important of our decade. His subject was Vietnam.
His hope was to rally the American people to see the conflict
through to a lasting and just peace in the Pacific. For thirty-
two minutes, he reasoned with a nation that has suffered

almost a third of a million casualties in the longest war in its history.

When the President completed his address—an address that he spent weeks in preparing—his words and policies were subjected to instant analysis and querulous criticism. The audience of seventy million Americans—gathered to hear the President of the United States—was inherited by a small band of network commentators and self-appointed analysts, the *majority* of whom expressed, in one way or another, their hostility to what he had to say.

It was obvious that their minds were made up in advance. Those who recall the fumbling and groping that followed President Johnson's dramatic disclosure of his intention not to seek reelection have seen these men in a genuine state of nonpreparedness. This was not it.

One commentator twice contradicted the President's statement about the exchange of correspondence with Ho Chi Minh. Another challenged the President's abilities as a politician. A third asserted that the President was now "following the Pentagon line." Others, by the expressions on their faces, the tone of their questions, and the sarcasm of their responses, made clear their sharp disapproval.

To guarantee in advance that the President's plea for national unity would be challenged, one network trotted out Averell Harriman for the occasion. Throughout the President's address he waited in the wings. When the President concluded, Mr. Harriman recited perfectly. He attacked the Thieu government as unrepresentative; he criticized the President's speech for various deficiencies; he twice issued a call to the Senate Foreign Relations Committee to debate Vietnam once again; he stated his belief that the Vietcong or North Vietnamese did not really want a military take-over of South Vietnam; he told a little anecdote about a "very, very responsible" fellow he had met in the North Vietnamese delegation.

All in all, Mr. Harriman offered a broad range of gratuitous advice—challenging and contradicting the policies outlined by the President of the United States. Where the President had issued a call for unity, Mr. Harriman was encouraging the country not to listen to him.

A word about Mr. Harriman. For ten months he was America's chief negotiator at the Paris peace talks—a period in which the United States swapped some of the greatest military concessions in the history of warfare for an enemy agreement on the shape of a bargaining table. Like Coleridge's Ancient Mariner, Mr. Harriman seems to be under some heavy compulsion to justify his failures to anyone who will listen. The networks have shown themselves willing to give him all the air time he desires.

Every American has a right to disagree with the President of the United States, and to express publicly that disagreement.

But the President of the United States has a right to communicate directly with the people who elected him, and the people of this country have the right to make up their own minds and form their own opinions about a presidential address without having the President's words and thoughts characterized through the prejudices of hostile critics before they can even be digested.

When Winston Churchill rallied public opinion to stay the course against Hitler's Germany, he did not have to contend with a gaggle of commentators raising doubts about whether he was reading public opinion right, or whether Britain had the stamina to see the war through. When President Kennedy rallied the nation in the Cuban missile crisis, his address to the people was not chewed over by a round-table of critics who disparaged the course of action he had asked America to follow.

The purpose of my remarks tonight is to focus your attention on this little group of men who not only enjoy a right of instant rebuttal to every presidential address, but more importantly, wield a free hand in selecting, presenting and interpreting the great issues of our nation.

First, let us define that power. At least forty million Americans each night, it is estimated, watch the network news. Seven million of them view ABC; the remainder being divided between NBC and CBS. According to Harris polls and other studies, for millions of Americans the networks are the sole source of national and world news.

In Will Rogers' observation, what you knew was what you read in the newspaper. Today, for growing millions of Americans, it is what they see and hear on their television sets.

How is this network news determined? A small group of men, numbering perhaps no more than a dozen "anchormen," commentators and executive producers, settle upon the 20 minutes or so of film and commentary that is to reach the public. This selection is made from the 90 to 180 minutes that may be available. Their powers of choice are broad. They decide what forty to fifty million Americans will learn of the day's events in the nation and the world.

We cannot measure this power and influence by traditional democratic standards for these men can create national issues overnight. They can make or break—by their coverage and commentary—a moratorium on the war. They can elevate men from local obscurity to national prominence within a week. They can reward some politicians with national exposure and ignore others. For millions of Americans, the network reporter who covers a continuing issue, like ABM or Civil Rights, becomes in effect, the presiding judge in a national trial by jury.

It must be recognized that the networks have made important contributions to the national knowledge. Through news, documentaries and specials, they have often used their power constructively and creatively to awaken the public conscience to critical problems.

The networks made hunger and black lung disease national issues overnight. The TV networks have done what no other medium could have done in terms of dramatizing the horrors of war. The networks have tackled our most difficult social problems with a directness and immediacy that is the gift of their medium. They have focused the nation's attention on its environmental abuses . . . on pollution in the Great Lakes and the threatened ecology of the Everglades.

But it was also the networks that elevated Stokely Carmichael and George Lincoln Rockwell from obscurity to national prominence. Nor is their power confined to the substantive.

A raised eyebrow, an inflection of the voice, a caustic remark dropped in the middle of a broadcast can raise doubts in a million minds about the veracity of a public official or the wisdom of a Government policy.

One Federal Communications Commissioner considers the power of the networks to equal that of local, state and Federal governments combined. Certainly, it represents a concentration of power over American public opinion unknown in history.

What do Americans know of the men who wield this power? Of the men who produce and direct the network news—the nation knows practically nothing. Of the commentators, most Americans know little, other than that they reflect an urbane and assured presence, seemingly well informed on every important matter.

We do know that, to a man, these commentators and producers live and work in the geographical and intellectual confines of Washington, D.C., or New York City—the latter of which James Reston terms the "most unrepresentative community in the entire United States." Both communities bask in their own provincialism, their own parochialism. We can deduce that these men thus read the same newspapers, and draw their political and social views from the same sources. Worse, they talk constantly to one another, thereby providing artificial reinforcement to their shared viewpoints.

Do they allow their biases to influence the selection and presentation of the news? David Brinkley states, "objectivity is impossible to normal human behavior." Rather, he says, we should strive for "fairness."

Another anchorman on a network news show contends: "You can't expunge all your private convictions just because you sit in a seat like this and a camera starts to stare at you. . . . I think your program has to reflect what your basic feelings are. I'll plead guilty to that."

Less than a week before the 1968 election, this same commentator charged that President Nixon's campaign commitments were no more durable than campaign balloons. He claimed that, were it not for fear of a hostile reaction, Richard Nixon would be giving into, and I quote the commentator, "his natural instinct to smash the enemy with a club or go after him with a meat ax."

Had this slander been made by one political candidate about another, it would have been dismissed by most commentators as a partisan assault. But this attack emanated from the privileged sanctuary of a network studio and therefore had the apparent dignity of an objective statement.

The American people would rightly not tolerate this kind of concentration of power in Government. Is it not fair and relevant to question its concentration in the hands of a tiny and closed fraternity of privileged men, elected by no one, and enjoying a monopoly sanctioned and licensed by Government?

The views of this fraternity do *not* represent the views of America. That is why such a great gulf existed between how the nation received the President's address—and how the networks reviewed it.

As with other American institutions, perhaps it is time that the networks were made more responsive to the views of the nation and more responsible to the people they serve.

I am not asking for government censorship or any other kind of censorship. I am asking whether a form of censorship already exists when the news that forty million Americans receive each night is determined by a handful of men responsible only to their corporate employers and filtered through a handful of commentators who admit to their own set of biases.

The questions I am raising here tonight should have been raised by others long ago. They should have been raised by those Americans who have traditionally considered the preservation of freedom of speech and freedom of the press their special provinces of responsibility and concern. They should have been raised by those Americans who share the view of the late Justice Learned Hand that "right conclusions are more likely to be gathered out of a multitude of tongues than through any kind of authoritative selection."

Advocates for the networks have claimed a first amendment right to the same unlimited freedoms held by the great newspapers of America.

The situations are not identical. Where the New York *Times* reaches 800,000 people, NBC reaches twenty times that number with its evening news. Nor can the tremendous impact of seeing television film and hearing commentary be compared with reading the printed page.

A decade ago, before the network news acquired such dominance over public opinion, Walter Lippmann spoke to the issue:

There is an essential and radical difference [he stated] between television and printing . . . the three or four competing television stations control virtually all that can be received over the air by ordinary television sets. But, besides the mass circulation dailies, there are the weeklies, the monthlies, the out-of-town newspapers, and books. If a man does not like his newspaper, he can read another from out of town, or wait for a weekly news magazine. It is not ideal. But it is infinitely better than the situation in television. There, if a man does not like what the networks offer him, all he can do is turn them off, and listen to a phonograph.

"Networks," he stated, "which are few in number, have a virtual monopoly of a whole medium of communication." The newspapers of mass circulation have no monopoly of the medium of print.

"A virtual monopoly of a whole medium of communication" is not something a democratic people should blithely ignore.

And we are not going to cut off our television sets and listen to the phonograph because the air waves do not belong to the networks; they belong to the people.

As Justice Byron White wrote in his landmark opinion six months ago, "It is the right of the viewers and listeners, not the right of the broadcasters, which is paramount."

It is argued that this power presents no danger in the hands of those who have used it responsibly.

But as to whether or not the networks have abused the power they enjoy, let us call as our first witnesses, former Vice President Humphrey and the city of Chicago.

According to Theodore H. White, television's intercutting of the film from the streets of Chicago with the "current proceedings on the floor of the convention created the most striking and *false* political picture of 1968—the nomination of a man for the American presidency by the brutality and violence of merciless police."

If we are to believe a recent report of the House Commerce Committee, then television's presentation of the violence in the streets worked an injustice on the reputation of the Chicago police.

According to the Committee findings, one network in particular presented "a one-sided picture which in large measure exonerates the demonstrators and protesters." Film of provocations of police that was available never saw the light of day, while the film of the police response which the protesters provoked was shown to millions.

Another network showed virtually the same scene of violence—from three separate angles—without making clear it was the same scene.

While the full report is reticent in drawing conclusions, it is not a document to inspire confidence in the fairness of the network news.

Our knowledge of the impact of network news on the national mind is far from complete. But some early returns are available. Again, we have enough information to raise serious questions about its effect on a democratic society.

Several years ago, Fred Friendly, one of the pioneers of network news, wrote that its missing ingredients were "conviction, controversy and a point of view." The networks have compensated with a vengeance.

And in the networks' endless pursuit of controversy, we should ask what is the end value . . . to enlighten or to profit? What is the end result . . . to inform or to confuse? How does the on-going exploration for more action, more excitement, more drama, serve our national search for internal peace and stability?

Gresham's law seems to be operating in the network news. Bad news drives out good news. The irrational is more controversial than the rational. Concurrence can no longer compete with dissent. One minute of Eldridge Cleaver is worth ten minutes of Roy Wilkins. The labor crisis settled at the negotiating table is nothing compared to the confrontation that results in a strike—or, better yet, violence along the picket line. Normality has become the nemesis of the evening news.

The upshot of all this controversy is that a narrow and distorted picture of America often emerges from the televised news. A single dramatic piece of the mosaic becomes, in the minds of millions, the whole picture. The American who relies upon television for his news might conclude that the majority of American students are embittered radicals, that the majority of black Americans feel no regard for their country; that violence and lawlessness are the rule rather than the exception, on the American campus. None of these conclusions is true.

Television may have destroyed the old stereotypes—but has it not created new ones in their place?

What has this passionate pursuit of "controversy" done to the politics of progress through logical compromise, essential to the functioning of a democratic society?

The members of Congress or the Senate who follow their principles and philosophy quietly in a spirit of compromise are unknown to many Americans—while the loudest and most extreme dissenters on every issue are known to every man in the street.

How many marches and demonstrations would we have if the marchers did not know that the ever-faithful TV cameras would be there to record their antics for the next news show.

We have heard demands that senators and congressmen and judges make known all their financial connections—so that the public will know who and what influences their decisions or votes. Strong arguments can be made for that view. But when a single commentator or producer, night after night, determines for millions of people how much of each side of a great issue they are going to see and hear; should he not first disclose his personal views on the issue as well?

In this search for excitement and controversy, has more than equal time gone to that minority of Americans who specialize in attacking the United States, its institutions and its citizens?

Tonight, I have raised questions. I have made no attempt to suggest answers. These answers must come from the media men. They are challenged to turn their critical powers on themselves. They are challenged to direct their energy, talent and conviction toward improving the quality and objectivity of news presentation. They are challenged to structure their own civic ethics to relate their great freedom with their great responsibility.

And the people of America are challenged too . . . challenged to press for responsible news presentations. The people can let the networks know that they want their news straight and objective. The people can register their complaints on bias through mail to the networks and phone calls to local stations. This is one case where the people must defend themselves . . . where the citizen—not Government—must be the reformer . . . where the consumer can be the most effective crusader.

By way of conclusion, let me say that every elected leader in the United States depends on these men of the media. Whether what I have said to you tonight will be heard and seen at all by the nation is not *my* decision; it is not *your* decision; it is *their* decision.

In tomorrow's edition of the Des Moines *Register* you will be able to read a news story detailing what I said tonight; editorial comment will be reserved for the editorial page, where it belongs. Should not the same wall of separation exist between news and comment on the nation's network?

We would never trust such power over public opinion in the hands of an elected government—it is time we questioned it in the hands of a small and unelected elite. The great networks have dominated America's airwaves for decades; the people are entitled to a full accounting of their stewardship.

AN ADDRESS BEFORE THE INTERNATIONAL RADIO AND TELEVISION SOCIETY [3]

FRANK STANTON [4]

A few days after Vice President Spiro Agnew delivered his address at Des Moines on the mass media, Federal Communications Commissioner Nicholas Johnson declared in a speech at Iowa City that

> It is true . . . a handful of men control what the American people see of the world through their television screens but the answer is not to transfer this power from a handful of men in New York to a handful of men in the White House. The answer is to return this power to the people.

Without necessarily endorsing the polemics, Robert Lewis Shayon, a contributing editor of *Saturday Review,* yet believed that the debate which Mr. Agnew started should go on. "The public interest," Mr. Shayon remarked, "rests neither in a maintenance of the status quo nor in a contraction of it. It rests in a multiplication of the voices that have access to the medium, and in an escalation of the quality of all the messages." But many people, including some television executives, saw in the Vice President's speech unmistakable signs of political warfare against the media. Moreover, they feared that regulation and censorship might be lurking near the battle line.

One of the liveliest and earliest defenses of television's overall performance, especially in broadcast journalism, came from Frank Stanton on November 25, 1969. Speaking over radio (a videotape was sent out later) before an assembly of the International Radio and Television Society in New York City, the president of the Columbia Broadcasting System viewed the Vice President's remarks as a threat to the free dissemination of ideas and information.

> If these threats implicit in the developments of the past week are not openly recognized, unequivocally denounced and firmly resisted, freedom of communications in this country will suffer a setback that will not be

[3] Delivered before a meeting of the International Radio and Television Society in New York City, November 25, 1969. Text furnished by Mr. Stanton, with permission for this reprint.

[4] For biographical note, see Appendix.

limited to checking the freedom of television or to barring critical comment on Government policy. It will precipitate an erosion that will inevitably destroy the most powerful safeguard of a free society—free, unhampered and unharassed news media.

Repeating his conviction that radio and television should not be immune from criticism, Mr. Stanton continued:

We are *not* unaccountable. We are *not* clandestine. We have *no* end product that is not seen and judged by everyone. But such open criticism is a far cry from sharp reminders from high official quarters that we are licensed or that if we don't examine ourselves, we in common with other media "invite" the Government to move in.

The issues in this debate are sensitive. They defy pat analysis. As Frank K. Kelly remarks in a footnote to the second edition of the 1960 Occasional Paper "Who Owns the Air?" published by the Center for the Study of Democratic Institutions, "No one has found a way to keep the media under effective surveillance without raising the specter of censorship." Mr. Kelly reaffirmed his confidence in the proposal for an independent citizens' commission which would issue regular reports on the quality of the media's performances. If it could publicize its findings widely, "its effects could be beneficial to professional communicators in the media as well as to the people at large."

I am not here to defend broadcast journalism as being beyond all criticism. No one could have worked as long as I have in radio and television without realizing that we are far from perfect in carrying out our enormous responsibilities in broadcast journalism. We have never been satisfied with the job we are doing. We are not satisfied now. It is our continuing hope and our continuing effort to do better. We are concerned with what the press says of us. We are concerned with what our audiences write us. We are concerned with what our affiliates tell us. We do strive for objectivity, although it is not always easy to achieve. While freedom of the press is meaningless without the freedom to be wrong, we do try to be right. And I think that in the vast majority of cases we have succeeded.

Let me turn now to the events of the past few weeks that have commanded the attention of many of us. On November 3, the President of the United States delivered a much publicized and eagerly awaited speech presenting the Administration's position and plans on the war in Vietnam. That war has been the subject of one of the longest and most fervent public debates in all American history. Good, conscionable and dedicated men and women, from all sections of our society, have earnest and deeply felt differences as to its meaning, its conduct and its prospects. Fundamental questions of rightness and wrongness have disturbed our people as no other issue has in this century.

The President spoke for thirty-two minutes on all four nationwide television networks, four nationwide radio networks and scores of independent stations. Some 88 million people heard his words as they were conveyed, uninterrupted and in a place and under conditions of his own choosing. Following the President's address, each of the television networks provided comments by professionals analyzing the content of the speech. Participating were experienced newsmen, most of whom have performed similar functions for many years following the live broadcast of special events of outstanding significance. Since the participants were different on the four television networks, the comments of none of them were heard by the same huge audience that heard the President. One of the networks added to the expertise by presenting the views of a distinguished diplomat and public servant, who had held high posts in nine presidential terms, of both parties, prior to the present Administration. Another presented the comments of two United States senators, who took divergent views of the policy advocated in the speech.

In all this, nothing unprecedented had happened. Such comments have customarily been offered after most significant presidential appearances—State of the Union, inaugurals, United Nations addresses, press conferences, for example. And they usually have been more than mere bland recapitulations, which would serve little purpose, and have frequently called attention to emphases, omissions, unexpected matters of substance, long anticipated attitudes, changes of views, methods of advocacy or any other aspect of the speech. Such comments have been offered by enterprising news organizations since the dawn of the modern press and continued into the era of radio and television.

Following the President's speech and following the relatively brief comments made directly after it, the White House was deluged with telegrams and letters approving the President's speech, the White House reported, by an overwhelming margin. Two days later, the Gallup Survey reported that nearly four out of every five of those who heard it, approved the President's speech and the course that it advocated with regard to Vietnam.

Ten days after the President's speech, the second highest official in the Administration launched an attack on the television networks on the grounds that critical comments on Government policy as enunciated in a Presidential address might unduly influence the American people—even though, following such comments, the President received a 77 per cent vote of confidence from those who heard him on the issue discussed.

The Vice President also censured television network news for covering events and personalities that are jolting to many of us but that nevertheless document the kind of polarized society—not just here but throughout the world, whether or not there is television and whether it is controlled or free—in which, for better or worse, we are living. It is not a consensus society. It is a questioning, searching society—unsure, groping, running to extremes, abrasive, often violent even in its reactions to the violence of others. Students and faculties are challenging time-honored traditions in the universities. Young clergy are challenging ancient practices and even dogma of the churches. Labor union members are challenging their leaderships. Scientists, artists, businessmen, politicians—all are drawn into the fray. Frequently, because everyone is clamoring for attention, views are set forth in extreme terms.

As we do not propose to leave unreported the voice of the Vice President, we cannot in good conscience leave unreported any other significant voice or happening—whether or not it supports Government policy, whether or not it conforms with our own views, whether or not it disturbs the persuasions of any political party or bloc. But no healthy society and no governing authorities worth their salt have to fear the reporting of dissenting or even of hostile voices. What a healthy society and a self-respecting government do have to fear—at the price of their vitality if not of their life— is the suppression of such reporting.

To strengthen the delusion that, as a news medium, television is plunging the nation into collapse and can be deterred only by suppressing criticisms and by either withholding bad news or contriving a formula to balance it with good news, the Vice President's speech was replete with misinformation, inaccuracies and contradictions. To deal adequately with all of these on this occasion would take us through the afternoon, but let me note some of them by way of example, then move on to consider with you the context of the Vice President's speech so far as the actions and statements of other Administration officials are concerned and, finally, make some observations on the significance of this unhappy affair.

The Vice President began his indictment of November 13 with a monstrous contradiction. He asserted flatly that "no medium has a more profound influence over public opinion" than television. And yet he also claimed that the views of America have been very little affected by this "profound influence," when he said, "The views of the majority of this fraternity [i.e., television network news executives and editors] do not—and I repeat, not—represent the views of America." The Vice President can't have it both ways. If the views of the American people show "a great gulf" between how a speech is received by them and how it is treated in a broadcast, obviously the treatment of it has no material effect upon their opinion. Even the premise of the Vice President's claim is proved wrong by the Gallup findings already mentioned.

The Vice President objected to the subjection of the words and policies of the President to "instant analysis and querulous criticism." The analysis, whatever its merits or failings, was hardly instant. Highly informed speculation about the content of the speech had gone on for days and even weeks. Copies were made available at least two hours in advance of the analysis, allowing at least as much time as most morning newspapers had before press time. If a professional reporter could not arrive at some meaningful observations under those circumstances, we would question his competence.

The Vice President took care—and the point should not be lost on us—to remind us that television is "enjoying a monopoly sanctioned and licensed by Government." A monopoly, by any definition I know, is the exclusive control of a product or a service by a single entity. Television news is broadcast in this country by four networks, all with different and fiercely competitive managements, producers, editors and reporters, involving hundreds of strongly individualistic people; by a dozen station groups, initiating and producing their own news broadcasts, and by hundreds of stations, producing their own news broadcasts wholly independent and distinct from those of any network they may otherwise be associated with. Moreover, it is estimated that, on the average day, 65 per cent more hours of viewing are devoted to station-originated news broadcasts than to network news broadcasts. In addition, there are 6717 radio stations in this country—the overwhelming majority without network affiliations. All this hardly represents monopolistic control.

The Vice President seems to maintain that the First Amendment applies differently to NBC from what it does to the New York *Times*, because NBC's audience is bigger and because television has more impact. That the First Amendment is quantitative in its applicability is a chilling innovation from a responsible officer of the Government. By this standard, the *Times* is less entitled to the protection of the Bill of Rights than the Des Moines *Register,* with a third of its circulation, and twice as entitled to it as the New York *Daily News,* which has double the *Times'* circulation. As for the impact of the television medium, it may be true that combined picture and voice give television a special force. On the other hand, print can be reread, it can be lingered over, it can be spread around, it can be consulted over and over again. Should, on the grounds of these advantages over television, the print media have less freedom?

The Vice President asked how many "marches and demonstrations" there would be if there were no television cameras. An elementary textbook in American history might prove instructive. There was no television to record the demonstrations against slavery; demonstrations against the Mexican War; demonstrations against the Civil War draft; demonstrations for women's suffrage; demonstrations for Prohibition; demonstrations for the League of Nations; demonstrations against child labor; demonstrations for economic justice. That there would be no disturbing news except for television is a canard as dangerous as it is egregious.

Now let us turn to the crucial issue raised by the Vice President.

Despite his complaints about how and what we report, the Vice President protested that he was not advocating censorship. He found it necessary, a week later, to repeat his protest three times in one paragraph. It is far more shocking to me that the utterances of the second-ranking official of the United States Government require such repeated assurances that he had in mind no violation of the Constitution than it is comforting to have them at all. Of course, neither he nor any of his associates are advocating censorship—which would never survive judicial scrutiny. But it does not take overt censorship to cripple the free flow of ideas. Was the Vice President's reference to television's being "sanctioned and licensed by Government" accidental and devoid of any point or meaning? Was his suggestion that "it is time that the networks were *made* [emphasis added] more responsive to the views of the nation" merely sloppy semantics and devoid of any notion of coercion?

Perhaps the Vice President, in his November 20 follow-up speech, was not referring to Government action, but only to a dialogue among citizens when he said,

When they [network commentators and some gentlemen of the New York *Times*] go beyond fair comment and criticism they will be called upon to defend their statements and their positions just as we must defend ours. And when their criticism becomes excessive or unjust, we shall invite them down from their ivory towers to enjoy the rough and tumble of public debate.

Who, in those sentences, will do the calling of these men to defend themselves, and before whom? Who is the "we" who shall do the inviting? And by whose standards will the limits of "fair comment" and "just criticism" be judged and who shall be the judges?

The ominous character of the Vice President's attack derives directly from the fact that it is made upon the journalism of a medium licensed by the Government of which he is a high-ranking officer. This is a new relationship in Government-press relations. From George Washington on, every Administration has had disputes with the press, but the First Amendment assured the press that such disputes were between equals, with the press beyond the reach of the Government. This all-important fact of the licensing power of life and death over the broadcast press brings an implicit threat to a government official's attacks on it, whether or not that is the intention and whether or not the official says he is speaking only as an individual.

But the Vice President does not seem to have been walking a lonely path in the direction of suppression and harassment:

Herbert G. Klein, the Administration's Director of Communications, revealed that, on November 4, the day after the President's speech, calls from White House offices went out to broadcast stations asking whether editorials were planned and, in Mr. Klein's words, "to ask them what they would say in their editorial comment."

In Washington, D.C., television stations were called by a member of the Subversive Activities Control Board, Paul O'Neil, requesting logs of news coverage devoted to support of and in opposition to the Administration's Vietnam policy. His wife, a Dade County official of the Republican Party, who specified her husband's official position, made the same request of Miami, Florida stations.

On November 4, the Chairman of the Federal Communications Commission, in unprecedented calls to the presidents of the three broadcasting companies with national television networks, requested transcripts of the remarks of their reporters and others who had commented on the speech, saying there had been complaints, the source of which he failed to specify—although two weeks later on sober second thought, he seemed to reverse himself when he signed a letter adopted by the full Commission finding that the comments made on the networks after the speech in no way violated its doctrine of fairness.

A special counsel to the President, Clark R. Mollenhoff, said that the speech "was developed by various White House aides," adding "if you are asking me, 'does it reflect the Administration's views,' the evidence is abundant that it does." The President's press secretary, Ronald Ziegler, agreed that a White House special assistant, Patrick J. Buchanan, "very well could have contributed some thoughts to the speech."

Mr. Klein, on November 16, said, "I think that any time any industry—and I include newspapers very thoroughly in this, as well as the networks—if you look at the problems you have today and you fail to continue to examine them, you do invite the Government to come in."

In my judgment, the whole tone, the whole content and the whole pattern of this Government intrusion into the substance and methods of the broadcast press, and indeed of all journalism, have the gravest implications. Because a federally licensed medium is involved, no more serious episode has occurred in Government-press relationships since the dark days in the fumbling infancy of this republic when the ill-fated Alien and Sedition Acts forbade criticism of the government and its policies on pain of exile or imprisonment.

In the context of this intimidation, self-serving disavowals of censorship, no matter how often repeated, are meaningless. Reprisals no less damaging to the media and no less dangerous to our fundamental freedoms than censorship are readily available to the Government—economic, legal and psychological. Nor is their actual employment necessary to achieve their ends; to have them dangling like swords over the media can do harm even more irreparable than overt action. If these threats implicit in the developments of the past week are not openly recognized, unequivocally denounced and firmly resisted, freedom of communications in this country will suffer a setback that will not be limited to checking the freedom of television or to barring critical comment on Government policy. It will precipitate an erosion that will inevitably destroy the most powerful safeguard of a free society—free, unhampered and unharassed news media.

This does not have to be the resolute intention of any person or group, any party or Government. We can wander unintentionally—all of us—into a lethal trap if we let our dissatisfaction with the handling of specific issues, which are variable, and of events, which are transitory, compromise our adherence to basic principles, which are constant. No permanent freedom was ever wisely exchanged for temporary popularity, for the popularity can be gone with changing political or social cycles and the freedom can be regained, if ever, only at fearful cost. And this is a truth that should be remembered by those who demand that our freedoms be preserved only when they agree with us, but who have been eager to restrict them whenever they disagree with us. You cannot side with restrictions or with bullying or with recriminations when they support your views and then oppose them when they differ, for they will rise up and haunt you long after your cause is lost or won.

The issue here is simple. Dwight D. Eisenhower said, "I believe the United States is strong enough to expose to the world its differing viewpoints . . . ." His successor, John F. Kennedy, said, "The men who create power make an indispensable contribution to the nation's greatness, but the men who question power make a contribution just as indispensable."

Criticism is an essential ingredient in that mix. It is central, not tangential, to a free society. It is always a free society's strength and often its salvation. Television itself is not and should not be immune to such criticism. As a matter of fact, it is the most criticized medium in the history of communications. Newspapers, magazines, academic groups, learned societies—who wouldn't dream of criticizing each other—criticize us every single day. Everyone has free access to what we do, and everyone sees us do it. We are *not* unaccountable. We are *not* clandestine. We have *no* end product that is not seen and judged by everyone. But such open criticism is a far cry from sharp reminders from high official quarters that we are licensed or that if we don't examine ourselves, we in common with other media "invite" the Government to move in.

The troubled pages of this country's history are writ dark with the death of liberty in those nations where the first fatal symptom of political decay was an effort to control the news media. Seldom has it been called censorship. Seldom is the word used except in denials. Always it has been "guidelines" in the name of national unity. And we might well ponder the fate of the unhappy roll of nations that had no regard for their freedoms or took them for granted or held them lightly.

As we meet here, thirty-nine nations in the world have a controlled press or a press that wavers uncertainly between control and freedom. This melancholy statistic might well be borne in mind by those of our own countrymen who, as the Vice President descends upon one part of the country to attack the journalists of another part, are moved by their temporary irritations to applaud their own ensnarement. In his speech of November 13, the Vice President turned to Learned Hand to support a proposition that would have been total anathema to the great judge. Let me, in conclusion, invoke Hand in more revealing words:

> Our democracy rests upon the assumption that, set free, the common man can manage his own fate; that errors will cancel each other by open discussion; that the interests of each when unguided from above, will not diverge too radically from the interests of all. . . .

I appreciate having had this opportunity to speak to you today in what all thoughtful people must regard as a critical period in the life of a free society and of the free communications without which it cannot exist.

NATIONAL CONSCIENCE AND THE ENVIRONMENT

A THEOLOGY OF THE EARTH [1]

René Dubos [2]

"A growing sense of responsibility of all men for each other cannot be expected to flow from the unlikely well of altruism, but from the desperately practical fact that our very survival as men depends on working together and helping each other." So wrote Dr. Roger Revelle, director of the Center for Population Studies at Harvard University, on the inseparability of human ecology and ethics. In this difficult job, Dr. Revelle views education as serving an important function in improving the quality of our environment. James E. Allen, Jr., former United States Commissioner of Education, shares this view: "The active involvement of an educational system in problems that pervade the lives of all will help to make the educational process more relevant and responsive."

The environmental crisis speaks in several voices: ethical-philosophical, humanistic, political. It deals at once with man's sense of relation to his surroundings, with his love for a natural world that is being altered sharply by people and technology, and with his willingness to pay the heavy price in dollars—not for survival alone but for the improvement of the quality of life, if indeed we do survive.

One of the best of the recent speeches on the subject was delivered by Dr. René Dubos on October 2, 1969, at the Smithsonian Institution in Washington, D.C. The world-renowned microbiologist and experimental pathologist at the Rockefeller University in New York developed the thesis that "we shall not be able to solve the ecological crisis until we recapture some kind of spiritual relationship between man and his environment."

Two basic theses emerge from Dr. Dubos' address. He enters a partial refutation of the view, rather widely held even in some theological circles, that the Christian tradition has given a kind of sanction to the desecration of the earth. Secondly, he develops the

[1] Speech delivered at the Smithsonian Institution, Washington, D.C., on October 2, 1969. Text furnished by Dr. Dubos and the Smithsonian Institution, with permission from both for this reprint.

[2] For biographical note, see Appendix.

argument that St. Benedict might more properly be regarded the patron saint of ecology than St. Francis. The latter represents the attitude of "passive worship"; the former, "creative intervention."

While the tone of Dr. Dubos' address is not lightheartedly optimistic, neither is it a testament of impending doom. It is, rather, a reaffirmation of faith in the resiliency and adaptability of man and nature.

Ladies and gentlemen, the title of this lecture would be pretentious if it did not express profound feelings that I experienced a few months ago at the time of the Apollo 8 mission. Shortly after the return to earth of Apollo 8 the science editor of the Columbia Broadcasting System, Earl Ubell, interviewed the crew over the CBS network. Through skillful and persistent questioning he tried to extract from the astronauts what had been their most profound impression during their trip through space. What turned out was that their deepest emotion had been to see the earth from space. The astronauts had been overwhelmed by the beauty of the earth as compared with the bleakness of space and the grayness of the moon.

On the whole, I have been rather skeptical concerning the scientific value of the man-in-space program. But, while listening to the Apollo 8 crew, I became interested in that effort because I felt that it would pay unexpected dividends —namely, make us objectively aware, through our senses as it were, of the uniqueness of the earth among other bodies in the sky.

The incredible beauty of the earth as seen from space results largely from the fact that our planet is covered with living things. What gives vibrant colors and exciting variety to the surface of the earth is the fact that it is literally a living organism. The earth is living by the very fact that the microbes, the plants, the animals, and man have generated on its surface conditions that occur nowhere else, as far as we know, in that part of the universe that we can hope to reach. The phrase "theology of the earth" thus came to me from the Apollo 8 astronauts' accounts of what they had seen from their space capsule, making me realize that the earth is a living organism.

My presentation will be a mixture of the emotional response of my total being to the beauty of the earth, and of my mental processes as a scientist trying to give a rational account of the earth's association with living things. The phrase "theology of the earth" thus denotes for me the scientific understanding of the sacred relationships that link mankind to all the physical and living attributes of the earth.

I shall have to touch on many different topics because I want to convey my belief that we have collectively begun to engage in a kind of discovery of ourselves—who we are, where we belong, and where we are going. A few lines from T. S. Eliot in his poem *Four Quartets* seems to me the ultimate expression of what I shall try to express emotionally and to analyze scientifically:

> We shall not cease from exploration
> And the end of all our exploring
> Will be to arrive where we started
> And know the place for the first time. [3]

All archaic peoples, all ancient classical cultures, have practiced some form of nature religion. Even in our times a large number of isolated, primitive tribes in Australia, in Africa, and in South America still experience a feeling of holiness for the land in which they live. In contrast, respect for the earth and for nature has almost completely disappeared from industrialized people in most of the countries that have accepted the ways of Western civilization.

Primitive religion, with its sense of holiness of the environment, was always linked with magic. It is easy to understand how there can be links between primitive religious beliefs and the attempts to control nature through the mysterious influences of the world. Even though they always have coexisted among primitive people, religion and magic represent two very different kinds of attitudes.

[3] The lines from "Little Gidding" from *Four Quartets* by T. S. Eliot are quoted by permission of Harcourt Brace Jovanovich, Inc.

In the words of the anthropologist Malinowsky: "Religion refers to the fundamental issues of human existence while magic turns round specific, concrete and practical problems."

Most of my remarks this evening will be based on the conviction that the ecological crisis in the modern world has its root in our failure to differentiate between the use of scientific technology as a kind of modern magic and what I shall call modern religion, namely, knowledge as it relates to man's place in the universe and, especially, his relation to the earth.

All ancient peoples personified a locality or a region with a particular god or goddess that symbolized the qualities and the potentialities of that place. Phrases such as "the genius of the place" or "the spirit of the place" were commonly used in the past. All followers of ancient cultures were convinced that man could not retain his physical and mental health and fulfill his destiny unless he lived in accordance with the traditions of his place and respected the spirit of that place. I believe it was this attitude that helped ancient peoples to achieve rich and creative adjustment to their surroundings. Now you may say: "Spirit of place; genius of place? This is no longer for us. We are far too learned and sophisticated."

Yet, rationalistic and blasé as we may be, we still feel, deep in our hearts, that life is governed by forces that have their roots in the soil, in the water, and in the sky around us. The last part of Lawrence Durrell's book *Spirit of Place* deals with this very topic. There is not one among us who does not sense a deep meaning in phrases such as "the genius of New England" or "the spirit of the Far West." We still sense that there is some kind of uniqueness to each place, each location, which gives it a very special meaning in our minds. But while we pine for the sense of holiness in nature, we do not know how to introduce this sense in our social structure. I am convinced that this has much to do with the ecological crisis.

I am not the first to express the feeling that we shall not be able to solve the ecological crisis until we recapture some

kind of spiritual relationship between man and his environment. Some two years ago, for example, the learned American scholar Lynn White, Jr., a professor at the University of
California in Los Angeles, delivered before the American
Association for the Advancement of Science a special lecture
titled "The Historical Roots of Our Ecologic Crisis." This
lecture must strike a very sensitive chord in the minds of
Americans because it has been reproduced again and again
in several journals—ranging from *The Oracle,* the organ of
the hippie movement in San Francisco, to the plush magazine *Horizon.* Among the many interesting and important
things White says, I single out a particular item with which
I disagree in part. He stated that, in his opinion, the lack of
reverence for nature on the part of modern industrial man,
especially in the United States, and the desecration of nature by technology are consequences of biblical teachings.
He traced them to the first chapter of Genesis in which it is
said that man and woman were given the right and the duty
to replenish the earth, subdue it, and have dominion over all
living things. According to White, this biblical teaching has
had such a profound and lasting influence on Western civilization that it has made modern man lose any feeling for
nature and to be concerned only with the conquest of nature
for his own benefit. Also, White sees no hope of retracing
our steps through science and technology because both exemplify the authority expressed in that statement in the first
chapter of Genesis. The only solution to the ecological crisis,
therefore, is to try to recapture the worshipful attitude that
the monks of the Franciscan order had toward nature in the
thirteenth century. The last sentence of White's lecture is, if
my memory serves me right, "I propose Francis as a patron
saint for ecologists."

All of us have some kind of sentimental, romantic sympathy with Lynn White's thesis. All of us are happy that
there have been practical expressions of this attitude in the
development of the national parks and in the attempts to
preserve as much wildlife as possible. By preserving the state

of certain wilderness areas, with their animals and plants, their rocks and marshes, mankind symbolizes that it has retained some form of respect for the natural world. In passing, it is not without interest that the United States—the country which has certainly been the most successful and has done the most toward achieving dominion over the earth through technology—is also the one country which is doing the most to save some fragments of wilderness. I wonder at times whether Glacier Park and Monument Valley do not represent a kind of atonement for God's own junkyard.

Despite my immense admiration for Lynn White's scholarship, I find it difficult to believe that the Judeo-Christian tradition has been as influential as he thinks in bringing about the desecration of the earth. One does not need to know much history to realize that the ancient Chinese, Greek, and Moslem civilizations contributed their share to deforestation, to erosion, and to the destruction of nature in many other ways. The goats of primitive peoples were as efficient as modern bulldozers in destroying the land. In any case, the Judeo-Christian attitude concerning the relation of man to nature is not expressed only in the first chapter of Genesis. The second chapter of Genesis states that man, after he had been placed in the Garden of Eden, was instructed by God to dress it and to keep it—a statement which has ecological implications. To dress and keep the land means that man must be concerned with what happens to it.

Man is rarely, if ever, just a worshiper of nature, a passive witness of its activities. He achieved his humanness by the very act of introducing his will into natural events. He became what he is while giving form to nature. For this reason I believe that ecologists should select St. Benedict as a much truer symbol of the human condition than Francis of Assisi. Most of you probably know little about St. Benedict, perhaps even less about the history of the Benedictine order. So allow me to elaborate on them for a few minutes because they represent a topic that is crucial to my personal attitude toward conservation.

St. Benedict created the first great monastery in the Western world on Monte Cassino, in Italy, in the sixth century. He must have been a wise man, because when he formulated the rules of conduct for Monte Cassino—rules which became a model for monastic life all over the world—he decided that the monks should not only pray to God but also should work. Moreover, he urged that the monastery be self-sufficient. The rule of work and the need for self-sufficiency led the Benedictine monks to master a multiplicity of practical arts, especially those relating to building and to architecture. The monks learned to manage the land in such a manner that it supplied them with food and clothing, and in such a manner that it retained its productivity despite intensive cultivation. Moreover, they developed an architecture which was lasting, well-suited to the country in which they lived as well as to their activities, and which for these reasons had great functional beauty. Those of you who have traveled over the world know that the Benedictine monasteries are marvels of medieval architecture.

It seems to me that the Benedictine rule implies ecological concepts which are much more in tune with the needs of the modern world than is the worshipful attitude of St. Francis. Perhaps most influential among the monks who followed the Benedictine rule were those of the Cistercian order. For reasons that I shall not discuss, the Cistercians established their monasteries in the lowlands and swamps; consequently, they had to learn to drain the land, and therefore they learned to use water power. And, through these technological practices, they converted areas of swamps and forests (that were not suitable for human habitation because of the prevalence of malaria) into wonderful fertile land which now makes up much of Europe's countryside.

If I have talked so long about St. Francis and St. Benedict it is not to give you a course in the history of medieval religion. Rather it is to illustrate two contrasting—but, I believe, equally important—attitudes toward nature: on the one hand, passive worship; on the other, creative intervention.

I have no doubt that the kind of worship symbolized by St. Francis helps man to retain his sanity by identifying himself with the totality of creation from which he emerged. Preserving the wilderness and all forms of wildlife is essential not only for esthetic and moral reasons but also for biological reasons.

Unfortunately, it will become increasingly difficult in the modern world to protect the wilderness from human use. In fact, no longer can there be any true wilderness. No fence is tight enough to shut out radiation clouds, air and water pollution, or noise from aircraft. Some ten or twenty years ago we could still escape from the insults of technological civilization by moving to the Rocky Mountains, to the Greek islands, or to the islands of the Pacific Ocean, but now the national parks and the isolated islands are almost as crowded and as desecrated as Coney Island. The only solution left to us is to improve Coney Island. In his short novel *Candide,* Voltaire pointed out that Candide discovered at the end of his adventures that the surest formula for happiness was to cultivate one's own garden. I believe that our Garden of Eden will have to be created in our own backyards and in the hearts of our cities. Just as the Benedictine monasteries had to apply, although empirically, ecological principles so as to remain self-supporting and viable, so must we learn to manage the earth in such a manner that every part of it becomes pleasant.

The achievements of the Cistercian monks serve to illustrate another aspect of modern ecologic philosophy. As I mentioned before, the swamps in which they established their monasteries were unfit for human life because of insects and malaria. But monastic labor, skill, and intelligence converted these dismal swamps into productive agricultural areas, many of which have become centers for civilization. They demonstrate that transforming of the land, when intelligently carried out, is not destructive but, instead, can be a creative art.

My speaking of medieval times in Europe was not meant to convey the impression that only then have there been great achievements in the management of the land. One need only look at the Pennsylvania Dutch country to see a striking demonstration of land that has been created out of the forest, that became highly productive, and that has been well preserved. One could cite many similar feats all over the world. But the tendency at present is to determine the use of lands and waters, mountains and valleys, only on the basis of short-range economic benefits. And yet one can safely assert that sacrificing ecological principles on the altar of financial advantage is the road to social disaster, let alone esthetic degradation of the countryside. I shall now present a few remarks about how we can create land. By this I mean taking nature as it is presented to us and trying to do with it something which is both suitable for human life and for the health of nature.

To do this it is essential that we identify the best "vocation" for each part of our spaceship. In Latin the word for "vocation" refers to the divine call for a certain kind of function. I wish we could apply this word, and indeed I shall apply it, to the different parts of the earth because each part of the earth has, so to speak, its vocation. It is our role as scientists, humanists, and citizens, and as persons who have a feeling for the earth, to discover the vocation of each part of it.

Certain parts of the earth, like certain persons, may have only one vocation. For example, there may be only one kind of thing that can be done with the Arctic country; there may be only a limited range of things that can be done with certain tropical lands. But in practice most places, like most persons, have several vocations, several options, and this indeterminism adds greatly to the richness of life. To illustrate with a few concrete examples what I have in mind, I ask that you consider what has happened to the primeval forest in the temperate parts of the world. I am not going to speak about the tropics, I am only going to speak of western Europe and the United States—the two parts of the world that I know best.

Much of the primeval forest in temperate countries has been transformed into farmland, but what is interesting is that each part of this primeval forest transformed into farmland has acquired its own agricultural specialization, social structure, and esthetic quality. On the other hand, the temperate forest need not become agricultural land. In Scotland and eastern England such lands progressively were transformed into moors—the famous moor country of the Scottish Highlands and eastern England. This happened largely through lumbering activities and also through the sheep grazing of the Benedictine monks. The moors are not very productive from the agricultural point of view, but their charm has enriched the life of Great Britain and played a large part in literature. In North America, much of the primeval forest was transformed into prairie country as a result of the fires set by the preagricultural Indians. The prairies have now been converted in large part into agricultural land, but they have left a lasting imprint on American civilization.

I have quoted a few transformations of the land from one ecological state to another which have been successful, but I hasten to acknowledge that many other such transformations have not been as successful. Much of the country around the Mediterranean has been almost destroyed by erosion, and very little is left of the famous cedars of Lebanon. The transformation from one ecological state to another has given desirable results, especially where it has occurred slowly enough to be compatible with adaptive processes either of a purely biological nature or when it involved the adaptation of man to the new conditions. This is the case for the moors in Great Britain. In this case the creation of romantic moors out of forest land took a thousand years, so there was a chance for all the adjustments that always occur in nature, when there is enough time, to come about. Contrast this with what happened in many parts of the United States where massive and hasty lumbering has been responsible for ghost towns and for eroded land.

From now on most of the transformations of the earth's surface will occur so rapidly that we may often create those terrible situations resulting in erosion and destruction of the land. It therefore is urgent that we develop a new kind of ecological knowledge to enable us to predict the likely consequences of massive technological intervention, and to provide rational guides as substitutes for the spontaneous and empirical adjustments that centuries used to make possible.

I have spoken so far chiefly of the transformations of the forest into new ecological structures that have economic value. But utilitarian considerations are only one aspect of man's relation to the earth. The widespread interest in the preservation of wildlife and primeval scenery is sufficient evidence that man does not live by bread alone and wants to retain some contact with his distant origins. In practice, however, the only chance that most people have to experience and enjoy nature is by coming into contact with its humanized aspects—cultivated fields, parks, gardens, and human settlements. It is, of course, essential that we save the redwoods, the Everglades, and as much wilderness as possible, but it is equally important that we protect the esthetic quality of our farmland, and to use this image again, that we improve Coney Island.

I wish there were time to discuss at length the factors that make for a beautiful landscape. Clearly, there is a kind of magic splendor and magnitude which gives a unique quality to certain landscapes. The Grand Canyon, the Painted Desert, and Niagara Falls are examples of scenery to which man's presence never adds anything, and may detract a great deal. In most cases, however, the quality of the landscape consists, in a sense, of fitness between man and his surroundings. This fitness accounts for most of the charm of ancient settlements, not only in the Old World but in the New World as well. The river villages of the Ivory Coast in Africa, the Mediterranean hill towns, the pueblos of the Rio Grande, the village greens of New England, and all the old cities so well organized around peaceful rivers represent many different types of landscapes that derive their quality not so much from topographical or climatic peculiarities as from an intimate association between man and nature.

Among the many factors that play a role in the sense of identification between man and nature, let me just mention in passing how history and climate condition the architecture and the materials of dwellings and churches. Also, how the climate determines the shape and the botany of gardens and parks.

The formal gardens of Italy and France didn't just happen through accidents or through the fancy of some prince or wealthy merchant. These wonderful parks and gardens were successful because they fitted very well into the physical, biological, and social atmosphere of Italy and France at the time of their creation. Such formal parks and gardens also flourished in England, especially during the seventeenth century, but the English school achieved its unique distinction by creating an entirely different kind of park. The great and marvelous English parks of the late seventeenth and eighteenth centuries were characterized, as we all know, by magnificent trees grouped in meadows and vast expanses of lawn. This style was suited to the climate of the British Isles, to the abundance of rain, and to the fact that insolation is sufficiently limited to permit certain types of growth. In France many attempts were made in the eighteenth century to create gardens and parks in the English style. Except in a few cases, however, English-type parks and gardens were not very successful in France.

On this topic, there is an interesting letter of Horace Walpole, who was one of the prophets of the English landscape school. He traveled in France and after his return he expressed a critical opinion of the attempts to duplicate the English park on the Continent. "The French will never have lawns as good as ours until they have as rotten a climate," he wrote in a letter. This witticism expresses the biological truth that landscape styles can be lastingly successful only if they are compatible with the ecological imperatives of the countries in which they develop. This is what Alexander Pope summarized in his famous line, "In everything respect the genius of the place." The word "genius" here express the total characteristics and potentialities of a particular area.

We should have Horace Walpole's phrase in mind when we look at what is being done in our large cities toward creating parks and gardens. Just as the climate in France cannot produce the green magnificence of the English parks, so in general the atmosphere in most of our large cities is unable to support most plant species. This does not mean that plant life is out of place in our cities, only that much more effort should be made to identify and propagate for each particular city the kinds of trees, flowers, and ground cover that can best thrive under its own particular set of climatic and other constraints. When I look on New York City parks and notice how their ordinary grass can appear so pathetic, and when I see how monotonous row after row of plain trees can be, I feel that botanists and foresters should be encouraged to develop other plant species congenial to urban environment. This is a wonderful field for plant ecologists because, in the very near future, pioneers of plant ecology are likely to be much more needed in the city than in the wilderness.

To summarize my remarks, let me restate that the "genius" or the "spirit of the place" is made up of all the physical, biological, social, and historical forces which, taken together, give uniqueness to each locality. This applies not only to the wilderness but also to human settlements—Rome, Paris, London, Hamburg, New York, Chicago, San Francisco —and I have selected these cities as representatives of very different types. Each of these cities has a genius that transcends its geographical location, commercial importance, and population size. The great cities of the world contribute to the richness of the earth by giving it the wonderful diversity that man adds to the diversity of nature. The "genius of the place" will be found in every part of the world if we look for it.

In the final analysis the theology of the earth can be expressed scientifically in the form of an enlarged ecological concept. Since this theology will be formulated by human minds it inevitably will involve man's interplay with nature. We certainly must reject the attitude which asserts that man is the only value of importance and that the rest of nature can be sacrificed to his welfare and whims. But we cannot escape, I believe, an anthropocentric attitude which puts man at the summit of creation while still a part of it. Fortunately, one of the most important consequences of enlightened anthropocentricism is that man cannot effectively manipulate nature without loving nature for her own sake. And here I shall have to summarize a set of complex biological concepts in the form of general and dogmatic statements which, I hope, will convey to you some feeling of what I would have liked to state more scientifically.

It is not just a sentimental platitude to say that the earth is our mother. It is biologically true that the earth bore us and that we endanger ourselves when we desecrate her. The human species has been shaped biologically and mentally by the adaptive responses it has made to the conditions prevailing on the earth when the planet was still undisturbed by human intervention. Man was shaped biologically and mentally while responding to wild nature in the course of his evolution. The earth is our mother not only because she nurtures us now but especially because our biological and mental being has emerged from her, from our responses to her stimuli.

Furthermore, the earth is our mother in more than an evolutionary sense. In the course of our individual development from conception to death, our whole being is constantly influenced by the stimuli that reach us from the environment. In other words, we constantly are being modified by the stimuli that reach us from nature and also from what

we have done to the earth. To a great extent, we therefore
come to reflect what we create. I shall restate here a phrase
of Winston Churchill's that I quoted two years ago in this
very room: "We shape our buildings and afterward our
buildings shape us."

This means that everything we create, good and bad,
affects our development and, more importantly, affects the
development of children. In his *Notes of a Native Son* James
Baldwin expressed even more vividly the influence of our
environment on our biological and mental characteristics.
Here are three phrases:

> We cannot escape our origins however hard we try, those
> origins which contain the key, could we but find it, to all that we
> later become.

> It means something to live where one sees space and sky, or
> to live where one sees nothing but rubble or nothing but high
> buildings.

> We take our shape within and against that cage of reality be-
> queathed us at our birth.

In the light of the remarks that I have presented to you,
I have come to a sort of general philosophy about the meaning of the word "conservation"; and it is with a brief statement of this philosophy that I end my presentation. Conservation programs, whether for wilderness or for man-made
environments, usually are formulated and conducted as if
their only concern were to the human species and its welfare.
Yet they can be effective only if they incorporate another
dimension, namely, the earth and her welfare. This is not
sentimentality but hard biological science. Man and the
earth are two complementary components of an indivisible
system. Each shapes the other in a wonderfully creative sym-
biotic and cybernetic complex. The theology of the earth
has a scientific basis in the simple fact that man emerged
from the earth and then acquired the ability to modify it
and shape it, thus determining the evolution of his own
future social life through a continuous act of creation.

THE ENVIRONMENT:
CAN MAN PROSPER AND SURVIVE? [3]

Edmund S. Muskie [4]

"A disease has infected our country. It has brought smog to Yosemite, dumped garbage in the Hudson, sprayed DDT in our food, and left our cities in decay." So read the opening lines of an environmental teach-in announcement in early January 1970, proclaiming April 22 Earth Day. The metaphor was aptly chosen. Environmental deterioration is a malady for which the cure is neither completely understood nor easy to apply. But the massive teach-ins conducted in several thousand schools, colleges and universities helped to alert the nation to the growing severity of the illness and the mounting hazards we will face if we rely upon little more than apathy to cure the distress.

Thanks in substantial measure to Senator Gaylord A. Nelson of Wisconsin, "father of the environmental teach-in," the words "environment" and "ecology" have taken on magical qualities, somewhat to the amazement of scholars and societies that have been promoting these causes for years. This is not to disparage the current concern for man and his surroundings; it is, rather, to rejoice in it—not as a novelty, however, but as an imperative which has but recently been forced into public consciousness. The jeremiad of old sounded the sorrowful note: "I beheld the earth, and, lo, it was without form, and void." It sounds again.

Senator Edmund S. Muskie of Maine is one of the nation's most articulate and persistent spokesmen for the development of a true "environmental conscience." A possible front-runner for the Democratic presidential nomination in 1972, Mr. Muskie is a prime mover for environmental legislation. He is an indefatigable speaker for the cause—in the Senate, on the college campuses, and from the public platform. The speech education profession has a special interest in his oratory. He was trained at Bates College under the direction of Brooks Quimby. Reportedly, Mr. Muskie believes in retrospect that his concern for "the rational, analytical approach to problems" is traceable to this early instruction.

[3] Speech delivered at a meeting of the Magazine Publishers Association in Chicago, Illinois, January 15, 1970. Text furnished by Senator Muskie, with permission for this reprint.

[4] For biographical note, see Appendix.

At the University of Michigan Environmental Teach-In on March 13, 1970, he urged the students to continue their efforts through a Citizens' Lobby which

> could voice effective demands for tough legislation. It could support candidates for public office who have shown a continuing commitment to strong environmental legislation. And it could bring pressure to bear to spend the money that must be spent.

Mr. Muskie approaches the environmental crisis as a practical, political matter. He is mindful that linguistic gloss, however necessary for developing national concern, is not enough. Substantial sums of money are needed and certain economic realities must be faced. It is good, therefore, to examine an address which deals, among other things of course, with dollars and cents. There is, as Edwin L. Dale, Jr., of the New York *Times* staff, once remarked, an "economics of pollution." And the stern fact is that "growth of production is the basic cause of pollution." Moreover, "anyone who wants us to go back to the ax, the wooden plow, the horse carriage and the water wheel is not only living a wholly impossible dream, he is asking for a return to a society in which nearly everybody was poor."

Mr. Muskie faces these dilemmas candidly. In his speech of January 15, 1970, before a meeting of the Magazine Publishers Association in Chicago, he spelled out the nature of the environmental threat, indicated what legislation had been enacted (he is the author of much of it), regretted the present Administration's indecision in promoting major programs, and made a final appeal for recognition of a simple but often conveniently forgotten fact:

> The problems of . . . pollution will not be solved by picking up the rhetoric of antipollution concerns and then assigning the control of pollution to those responsible for the support or promotion of pollution activities.
> The focus of our environmental protection must be man —man today, man tomorrow, and man in relation to all the other forms of life which share our biosphere.

In their conceit adults often forget that the very young have a stake, perhaps even larger than theirs, in environmental improvement. It is heartening, therefore, to learn that the second-graders who give up their play period to clean the school grounds are also actively on the side of the angels. A letter from one of these youngsters to a Texas legislator strikes a simple, humane note:

I . . . try my best to keep the world clean. And I hope
everyone is too. The noise, air, and water pollution is
ugly. But, I can live.

Let us hope that we can share this little girl's faith.

Adlai Stevenson once said: "It is the urgent duty of a
political leader to lead, to touch if he can the potentials of
reason, decency, and humanism in man, and not only the
strivings that are easier to mobilize."

Today is the anniversary of Martin Luther King's birth.
His death was a setback for the forces of reason, decency and
humanism. It came at a time—still with us—when men tended
to yield to "strivings that are easier to mobilize"—fear, suspicion, prejudice, hatred.

It would be well to pause a moment to consider a thought
expressed by Einstein: "Many times a day I realize how much
my own outer and inner life is built upon the labors of my
fellow men, both living and dead, and how earnestly I must
exert myself in order to give in return as much as I have
received."

It is a thought which has its application as well to the
question of man's relationship to his environment.

At least since Franklin's time, men have debated the
blessings and the dangers of technological progress.

In 1843 Thoreau said of machines: "They insult nature.
Every machine, or particular application, seems a slight outrage against universal laws. How many fine inventions are
there which do not clutter the ground?"

Unhappily, perhaps, a different thought prevailed—one
expressed in 1909 by city planners Daniel Burnham and
Edward H. Bennett in these words: "The rapidly increasing
use of the automobile" would promote "good roads and
[revive] the roadside inn as a place of rest and refreshment.
With the perfection of this machine and the extension of
its use, out of door life is promoted, and the pleasures of
suburban life are brought within reach of multitudes of
people who formerly were condemned to pass their entire
time in the city."

With the benefit of hindsight, which view would we say was nearer the truth?

This much—surely—we know: that material affluence exacts a price of the natural environment man needs to survive.

This much more we should know: that unless we change our ways, the price is one that threatens man's survival.

This, I believe, is the reason environmental protection has become such an important social and political issue.

It is important because the threat is real and present. It is important because it strikes at some cherished illusions about our society and about ourselves. It is important because the world which our children will inherit is in serious trouble.

The pollution problem is not new. Ancient societies sensed it. The Romans grappled with it. The British were plagued with it when they tried to use sea coal. Well over a century ago Henry Thoreau was warning us against damage to the natural resources of New England.

But until very recently, man has been willing to accept pollution as "the price of progress." Now he is not certain that "progress" is worth the price.

Lord Ritchie-Calder observed recently that "the great achievements of *Homo sapiens* become the disaster-ridden blunders of unthinking man—poisoned rivers and dead lakes, polluted with the effluents of industries which give something called 'prosperity' at the expense of posterity."

Americans, today, young and old, are putting more stock in posterity than in the general dream of prosperity. They have been frightened by the prospect of nuclear war and appalled by the destruction of conventional war. Their confidence has been undermined by the findings about cigarettes and health, the side effects of certain drugs, the long-term damage of pesticides and insecticides, and the potential hazards of diet sweeteners which are supposed to keep you slim and trim.

They have learned a great deal about these threats through the media from television specials and newspaper and magazine articles, and even from advertisements placed by companies eager to prove how concerned they are about the environment.

As always, men and women will lash out against the obvious threats to their health and well-being. They will attack nuclear power plants and oil refineries, paper mills and automobile factories, tanneries and steel mills. At the same time, unfortunately, very few will ask questions about their own demand for electrical energy, for fuel, for paper, for automobiles, shoes and steel products. Very few will question the damage they are causing as part of a consumption-oriented society.

We must understand that we cannot afford everything under the sun. Since our technology has reached a point in its development where it is producing more kinds of things than we really want, more kinds of things than we really need, and more kinds of things than we can really live with; the time has come to face the realities of difficult choices.

The time has come when we must say no to technological whims which pose a greater threat to the environment than we can control.

We have come a long way in alerting the public to the danger of pollution. We still have a long way to go in getting individuals to accept their own responsibility for improving the environment—whether they are industrialists, developers, public officials, or private citizens.

In 1963 the Congress enacted the Clean Air Act over complaints that "there is no need for the Federal Government to become involved in air pollution."

In 1965 we moved to establish Federal control over automobile emissions while the Department of Health, Education and Welfare argued that a mandatory program was premature.

In 1967 we enacted the Air Quality Act establishing a regional approach to air quality improvement and were told by private industry that there is not sufficient evidence to demonstrate a relationship between health and air pollution.

Much the same legislative history accompanies enactment of Federal water pollution control legislation. Even though fifteen million fish died last year from water pollution, even though water supplies are increasingly threatened, and even though demands for water recreation increasingly go unmet, industry leaders have resisted a minimal requirement to apply economic and technically feasible control technology for pollution abatement.

Very recently the soap and detergent industry contended that because it is not the only cause of lake eutrophication, it should not be asked to find substitutes for phosphates in its detergents.

The public is not prepared to accept such arguments any more. Neither is it prepared to accept empty political promises on environmental quality. And the public is right.

Too often our environmental quality legislation reminds us of unkept promises and unmet needs. We talked about $6 billion of Federal funds for community water pollution facilities and in 1966 the Senate voted that amount. The Congress finally agreed to $3.25 billion. But two Administrations have asked for only $620 million of the first $2 billion.

As the author of most of this legislation, I hope that new programs will be requested, that the Congress will respond, and that new commitments will be made. But I am concerned that new promises will be broken, because we are not prepared to back up those promises with the commitment of resources to the fight against pollution.

To those newly aroused about the dangers, let us make clear that the mere rhetoric of alarm is not enough.

To put it bluntly, talk will not be cheap if its objective is further delay.

We cannot expect to whip the public into a fervor of anticipation and not deliver the environmental improvement our words promise.

Statements of national policy, appointment of advisory councils, reorganization of Congress or the Federal bureaucracy, and talk of incentives are cake when the people of the United States, especially the young people, would like to see some bread.

ABC's William Lawrence put it this way in summing up the nation's domestic needs: It is time to "put our purse where we put our promises."

This is the critical issue on which the success or failure of an effort to control and improve environmental quality will be decided. There is a tendency to assume that programs to attack existing pollution problems do not exist. They do—but they have not been funded.

To date no substantive environmental program has received meaningful support from President Nixon or his Cabinet. The Administration's effort has been slogan-rich and action-poor. Rhetoric has taken us in one direction, while inaction has taken us in the other.

Let's look at the record.

Water pollution control demands are high. The Federal Government owes communities and states more than $760 million in due bills for projects now being built or completed, and new projects will need 2.3 billion Federal dollars this year. But this past year the Administration requested only $214 million of an authorized $1 billion. Eight hundred million dollars was voted by the Congress but indications are that nearly $600 million of these funds will be impounded.

Solid waste, responsible for numerous health and aesthetic problems, threatens to engulf us. Secretary of Health, Education, and Welfare Robert Finch testified to the critical nature of the nation's solid waste problem during hearings on pending bipartisan legislation—legislation which would move toward recovery, recycling and reuse of the vital resources which today the nation burns, buries or dumps. After providing an excellent critique of the immensity of the problem, he flatly opposed making available the funds required to fund and implement solutions.

A stirring State of the Union speech, based on thousands of man-hours of research on the problems of the environment will be just another *contribution* to environmental pollution if it does not include a firm commitment of manpower, money and back-up authority to attack the backlog of pollution problems and to give us the capacity to prevent a greater disaster.

I want to underscore the importance of dealing with today's problems while we attempt to head off the threats of tomorrow. Because of the romantic appeal of combating tomorrow's problems in their infancy, there will be a temptation to focus attention on the projected dangers at the expense of today's needs.

Romance is a necessary ingredient in motivating people to act, but it can turn to disillusionment if we find that we have protected ourselves against the dangers of DDT while our rivers and lakes have turned into cesspools.

We need an environmental policy which is designed to correct the abuses of the past, to eliminate such abuses in the future, to reduce unnecessary risks to man and other forms of life, and to improve the quality of our design and development of communities, industrial units, transportation systems and recreational areas. Such a policy must be carried out in the context of an increasing population which, because of the leisure and affluence available to it, will make greater demands on resources and the natural environment.

As a step toward implementing such a policy I have recommended the creation of a watch-dog agency responsible for Federal environmental protection activities. Such an agency must be independent of Federal operating programs and it must have authority to develop and implement environmental quality standards.

There are those who favor the creation of a Department of Natural Resources or a Department of Conservation to handle such functions. Whatever the merits of such a department to serve *other* purposes, such a move for these purposes would be a mistake, because it would ignore the fact that our environmental protection problem involves competition in the use of resources—a competition which exists today in the Department of the Interior and would exist in any department which must develop resources for public use.

The Department of Transportation is not the agency to determine air pollution control requirements for the transportation industry. The Atomic Energy Commission is not the agency to establish water pollution control requirements for nuclear power plants. The agency which sets environmental quality standards must have only one goal: protection of this and future generations against changes in the natural environment which adversely affect the quality of life.

The problems of environmental pollution will not be solved by picking up the rhetoric of antipollution concerns and then assigning the control of pollution to those responsible for the support or promotion of pollution activities.

The focus of our environmental protection effort must be man—man today, man tomorrow, and man in relation to all the other forms of life which share our biosphere. And man's environment includes the shape of the communities in which he lives, his home, his schools, his places of work, his modes of transportation and his society.

Our environmental concern must be for the whole man and the whole society, or else we shall find that the issue of environmental protection is another one of Don Quixote's windmills.

Last week I participated in hearings on our disaster relief program as it related to Hurricane Camille. Of all the lessons I learned from those hearings, one of the most important was the need to build better than we have when we have encountered a natural or man-made disaster.

The disaster of environmental destruction, which is all around us, should be turned into an opportunity to rebuild our society. We can make that opportunity if we reorder our priorities.

—The economic imbalance which has caused the population shifts which now so deeply trouble our American
cities

—The adequacy of housing and services both in urban
and rural America

—The availability of health services

—The conservation of natural resources and

—The availability of recreational opportunities in and
around our cities. . . .

All of these are high on the list of domestic priorities and
none of these can be said to be any less important or basically
more important than the crisis of the environment. They are,
indeed, a part of the environment.

If we see man as a part of his entire environment, and
if we see more clearly our relationship to each other, we may
be able to make America whole again.

It is the crisis of division and distrust in our society
which, left unresolved, will make achievement of our other
priorities meaningless.

We cannot live as two societies or four societies: and
government, state, local or Federal, cannot bring us together. Today is the anniversary of the birth of Dr. Martin
Luther King, who spent a lifetime trying to weld black and
white together and who was lost before he won. He gave
his life to avoid this deep division and to eliminate hatred
of man against his fellow man.

I think it is well to recommit ourselves today to the goals
set forth by Martin Luther King, and to make that commitment in the spirit of the American dream, which is not
simply affluence and physical comfort, but a society of
healthy men and women free to achieve their own potential.

THE POSITIVE POWER OF SCIENCE [5]

Glenn T. Seaborg [6]

If, as speculation has it, there are now more people in New York City than there were in all the earth seven thousand years ago, no special talent is needed to infer that the human state has become disturbingly complex. In recent years, science and technology have doubtless contributed to the ensnarement of man and to the creation of seemingly insoluble difficulties. It is easy, therefore, to put the blame for the anguish of our time on large, faceless scapegoats. And that is what has been done. Rightly or wrongly, science and technology are today's whipping boys. Both the rigor of the scientific process and the results and applications of experimental research are under scrutiny.

Accordingly, it is appropriate to hear again the voice of the high-level scientist; to find out how science relates to the abrasive facts of war, pollution, general malaise. Nobel Prize winner Glenn T. Seaborg provides us such insights. Experimentalist, teacher, administrator, and present chairman of the Atomic Energy Commission, he combines in his statements the hard, precise perceptions of the scientist with the warm compassion of the philosophical humanist.

The following speech was delivered in New York City on May 1, 1970, before the International Joint Conference of the American Geographical Society and the American Division of the World Academy of Art and Science. In the address he expressed a restrained optimism that the scientific forces which had contributed to the world's agonies could also help solve them.

A good companion piece to this address is Mr. Seaborg's "The Scientist As a Human Being" which was included in the 1964-1965 edition of REPRESENTATIVE AMERICAN SPEECHES.

To speak to such a distinguished gathering, and one that over the past few days has immersed itself in matters of such importance, is indeed a challenge. This has been a

[5] Address delivered at the International Joint Conference of the American Geographical Society and the American Division of the World Academy of Art and Science, in New York City, on May 1, 1970. Text furnished by Mr. Seaborg, with permission for this reprint.

[6] For biographical note, see Appendix.

conference with a difficult and most urgent task—that of considering "the environmental and social consequences of science and technology" and, in the light of these considerations, attempting to "formulate policy goals and strategies for the needs of man." Of course, the kind of thinking that has been responsible for initiating this conference and organizing its direction and content has been long overdue. Most of us, I am sure, realize that, whatever has been accomplished during these deliberations and discussions, we cannot be too self-congratulatory. There is a great segment of the public that would tell us we are "too late with too little." And a significant part of that group will go even further and say that we of the scientific community and our work are at the root of much of man's ills today.

Nevertheless, I am not here tonight to add to the despair and guilt of our times. I am not one who happens to believe that we can degrade the environment less by degrading man more. We are not going to save the earth merely by despising ourselves as its inhabitants any more than we are going to build a better society by belittling ourselves as individuals.

I think it is unfortunate—almost calamitous—that in the often sincere effort to establish a better perspective on our past errors and a sense of proportion about our present powers there are many who feel they have to go to the extremes of demeaning man, of denying reason and downgrading science. Tonight I plan to defend all three. I particularly want to speak up in behalf of science and urge that it rise to the crisis that faces it and man. In a sense it will be the success or failure of science—science epitomizing man's extended perception and power—that may well determine his survival as a species. But it is not science as we have used it in the past that will do the job. It must be science as part of a new human philosophy, as part of a new age of enlightenment that we are entering. And it is both the past shortcomings and successes of science that are moving us into that age. Let me explain.

What we are seeing today in all our social upheavals, in all our alarm and anguish over an environmental feedback and, in general, the apparent piling of crisis upon crisis to an almost intolerable degree, is not a forecast of doom. It is the birthpangs of a new world. It is the period of struggle in which we are making the physical transition from man to mankind—a mankind that will be an organic as well as a spiritual whole on this earth. I see this transition as a natural evolutionary process, a continuation of the growth and growing complexity of life on this planet. I do not believe that this growth is malignant in nature. It will not destroy itself by devouring its host or poisoning itself in its own waste. Neither will it self-destruct after delivering its message. Rather it will self-adjust through listening to and responding to that message—one that for all the static surrounding it is coming through quite clear.

I would like to touch on several ideas related to my admittedly broad and optimistic outlook for the future. In each case I hope to bring in the relationship of science and technology to the more general idea.

First, let me dwell on the subject of growth. This is something that until recently was a major value but of which we now seem to be developing a deadly fear. Both that growth and today's reactions to it, I believe, are natural and necessary. There seem to be many people today who, with no mean amount of eloquent hindsight, deplore the fact we did not, long before now, predict our population growth and our growing productivity with its accompanying waste, and somehow forecast our current environmental dilemma. Unfortunately, most great minds of the past foresaw only small segments of the evolving problem. And the values of the past were centered about unlimited growth because this seemed to be to the advantage of the individual and his society. In a world of seemingly endless physical frontiers, where the exploration and exploitation of these frontiers by new human creativity generated and fulfilled new human needs and values, few if any could think in terms of limits, balance and stability.

Many of us who today talk so glibly about our use of the atmosphere and oceans as "sinks," and who have embraced ecology almost as fervently as we have become embarrassed with economics, tend to overlook or forget the facts and feelings of the most recent past. It does little good to make scapegoats of our ancestors or of one or another segment of our society for the crises we face today. Our environmental crisis in particular could not have been theorized or accepted in the abstract before. It was an experiment that had to be lived in conjunction with the other problems of human growth that have evolved and which we must now move on to resolve. I think it was inevitable that man had to grow to this point. He is now entering what must be a period of tremendous maturity. And just as there is written within the genetic code some incipient biological mechanism that stops physical growth at a certain point in life so I believe there is within our evolving mankind a well-coded message that is now being released.

Before I go on to discuss some of what that message means, let me backtrack to discuss the role of science and technology in the growth to which I have referred.

It is obvious that for some people science and technology are among the best scapegoats of the time. They are said to be the cause of most of our ills today. By conquering disease and extending life they have been responsible for an explosion of population. By increasing productivity and raising living standards they have been responsible for depleting resources and polluting nature. By expanding knowledge and emphasizing efficiency, they have been responsible for deflating myths and diminishing man. And by placing enormous power in the hands of man they have brought him to the brink of his own destruction. The list of accusations is endless and it is not fashionable today to attempt to answer the charges or put the matter in perspective. It is more fashionable to dwell on man's relationship to the nat-

ural world, to lament that he is not more like the animal
life from which he descended and to wish for his return to
a simpler, perhaps more primitive, existence.

This approach may be more fashionable, it may even
contain a certain amount of wisdom we should heed, but it
is not the whole message we should be hearing. The major
part of that message, I believe, should tell us not to deny
our dependence on nature but neither to deny our differences
from what we left behind in our evolution. It is this recognition of what we are—with all its potential as well as its
shortcomings—and the emphasis on what we must and can
become that is important. The fact is that in this transitional period from tribal man to a truly organic mankind,
and to a world in which we can live in harmony with each
other and in balance with our global environment, we need
a new level of excellence in our science and technology and
a new degree of integration between them.

There is, no doubt, a great deal of pain and shock involved in this transitional period for we are breaking one
set of long-established natural bonds and forming new ones.
The whole process of change produces shock, reaction and
readjustment. There is always a tendency to revert back,
to flee from the new and challenging, before new understanding and confidence allow us to move ahead. We are
living through such times. We are experiencing what Alvin
Toffler refers to as "future shock," and it is often difficult to
sort out our movement and its direction. For example, take
note of the action and reaction of our youth as it resists
some change with an antirational thrust—and often a flight
from reality—while at the same time demanding realization
of a new level of idealism that can only be achieved through
change—change employing the highest form of rationality.

A similar dichotomy and flux exist in our confrontation
with environmental problems. Many feel the need for simplicity, limits and balance. Yet we know that what we must
do to accomplish the goals we express in these terms involves to some degree the mastery of a greater complexity,

new growth and a dynamic rather than static type of balance. We really do not want to freeze the world as it is now or go back to "the good old days." What we want, if I read correctly the ideals that so many of you—and so many deeply thinking and concerned people around the world—feel today, is a world far different than we have ever known it. Today—at this conference and at similar meetings that are being held and organized—we are struggling, fiercely but fruitfully I think, to clarify our conception of that world and work toward its realization. We must not weaken or lose heart in this struggle.

What will be the outcome when we begin to succeed? What will the evolution of this new mankind mean? And what will be some of the manifestations that it is taking place and succeeding?

Perhaps most important, we will see the elimination of war as an attempt to resolve human differences. It will not be only that war becomes untenable as a form of such resolution. Neither will it be only that through the wisest and fullest application of science and technology we will eliminate most of the physical insecurity and want at the root of war. What may be most significant as both a cause and effect in establishing world peace will be a sublimation of man's territorial instincts, and the aggressiveness that is tied to it, to a new feeling, one of the communality of man in the possession of the entire earth. Men are already in some measure sharing the earth through international travel, communication and exchange of resources. As this sharing is enhanced by a parallel releasing of the age-old bond of fear of scarcity—and adjustments in the economic system we have built to institutionalize that bond—we will begin to see the true meaning of the brotherhood of man materialize. And as this happens the tribal loyalty that Arthur Koestler has seen as the root of much of man's conflict will be broken and shift to a new global loyalty—a loyalty of man to all his fellowmen.

Concurrently with this establishment of world peace—and again as both a cause and effect of it—will be the closing of the chasms between the peoples of the world. Aurelio Peccei, Barbara Ward and many others have warned us that we cannot live in a world growing apart in the rate of development of its peoples. What I think we must, and will, see is a new concerted effort to raise the standard of living and productivity of the underdeveloped areas of the world while readjusting the growth of what many feel are becoming "overdeveloped" areas, harming themselves and others by some unwise management of their power and affluence. Anyone fully attuned to the problems of the world today can feel the need for this effort and readjustment. I think it is vitally important that we in scientific and technological fields do everything we can to encourage and work with those social and political forces that recognize this need and are trying to fulfill it. I will have more to say about such cooperative efforts in a moment.

Another manifestation of our evolving mankind will be the reduction, and eventual elimination, of environmental pollution. The organic mankind of which I have spoken could exist but momentarily on this earth if it were to act as a parasite or cancer. It must learn to exist as an integral and contributing part of the earth that up to now has supported it unquestioningly. This can only be achieved by the formulation and application of a whole new scientific outlook and new ecological-technological relationship. This relationship must be based on a nonexploitive, closed-cycle way of life that is difficult to conceive of in terms of the way we live today. We will have to achieve what René Dubos has referred to as a "steady-state world." We will have to think and operate in terms of tremendous efficiencies. We will have to work with natural resources, energy and the dynamics of the biosphere as a single system, nurturing and replenishing nature as she supports and sustains us. Such a system can be operated at various levels. A steady-state world does not have to be one in which mankind merely subsists and waits for natural evolution to take place. In fact, a steady-state world would be a challenge and stimulus to man's creative evolution—which I believe we should not deny is a natural process and which may be the highest form of natural evolution. Perhaps the organic global mankind which I have portrayed will be the acme of physical evolution on this planet. And I will not try to speculate beyond this point.

I have no doubt that many people envision the concept of such a complex, efficient and organic mankind as a nightmare—an anthill civilization in which individuals are mere automatons or mindless cells in an emotionless body. I do not agree with such thinking. What I see evolving is quite the opposite of this. It is a world in which the sphere of freedom of action and choice, individual creativity and sensitivity is enlarged by the growth and application of knowledge and by greater efficiency and organization. These elements buy time and provide freedom. It is ignorance, confusion and waste that enslave and eventually destroy.

Of course, new values and greater education must accompany the transition to this type of civilization. That is why I believe that the age of enlightenment we must enter must be one that combines scientific understanding with a new humanistic philosophy. We need both now to survive and grow.

What will be the role and direction of science in achieving this new age? I believe this conference offers us a good indication of both. But let me briefly sketch what I feel has been the movement of science and where it is going today.

Science, we might say, has become a victim of its own success. Or to put it more precisely, it has become a victim of its own single-minded success. I think this has happened in several ways. First, in going from the broad and general philosophy from which it originated into a growing number of more precise disciplines—each becoming more productive the narrower its focus became—science traded off wisdom for knowledge and, to some extent, knowledge for information.

In recent years this process has been reversed and we are now seeing the growth of interdisciplinary sciences and a striving for a more all-encompassing grasp of the physical world and even broader relationships such as you have been exploring in this conference. This type of growth is essential if science is to be the guiding force—as it must be—behind our evolving mankind. Science must grow stronger by continuing to nourish and improve its individual disciplines. We need the specific knowledge they offer. At the same time it must grow wiser through its correlation of knowledge. And it must be able to transmit its wisdom in the most effective way to society.

We have a tremendous task before us in humanizing the focus and feeling of science while at the same time organizing and rationalizing the forces of humanity. In recent years we have not been too successful in either of these directions. That is the reason why we have been faced, and are faced today, with a decline in the prestige of science, an anti-rational reaction on the part of many of our disillusioned youth, talk of the "eroding integrity of science" and even a feeling of guilt and despair in much of the scientific community. We must move away from all this. We must work toward a unification of the scientific spirit and a restoration of our self-confidence as well as a new degree of respect for science on the part of those who have lost faith and hope in it.

Let me offer some specific proposals as to ways we might accomplish this.

I think we should establish more international interdisciplinary conferences—such as the outstanding one we have been attending here—and more organizations that integrate our various disciplines, within and outside of the sciences. I believe these conferences and organizations should bring together for positive, constructive exploration, discussion and action participants of varied interests, opinions and talents—visionaries and realists, environmentalists and technologists, ecologists and economists, theorists and activists.

But the purpose of these meetings should not be that of many of the "confrontations" we are witnessing today. We should seek not the degraded power of polarization but the more beneficial strength of unity—that achieved through recognizing and working toward common goals.

In this regard I would like to see those scientists who in recent years have done a great service to man by calling attention to his environmental problems now contribute an even greater service by joining their colleagues in a concerted effort to solve those problems.

I think that out of such conferences as we have held here should come concrete programs or ideas that can be acted upon, as well as the broader policy-setting type of recommendations. We must give our activists something constructive to act upon and encourage the idea that many small positive measures can add up to a significant force. They can develop an important momentum and a spirit that in time can become overwhelming in its total effect.

I think that the information and programs generated at these conferences must be brought to the attention of the public and the world's political leaders more successfully. We have been very unsuccessful in communicating with the public, in bridging the gap between the Two Cultures. Now we must not only communicate, we must involve. We should particularly encourage the participation of youth in scientific and technical activities. Merely to decry their alienation, to speak of their immaturity or their unrealistic, "nonnegotiable" approach to achieving their ideals, is pointless— more than that, it is disastrous. We must at all levels engage them in the realities of life, not to blunt their ideals or enthusiasm, but for the purpose of capturing what is good and constructive in them, of harnessing their energy and creativity, of growing with them.

If some sparks must fly between the gap of our generations let us not use them to ignite conflagrations but rather to fire an engine of human progress. We in the scientific community in particular need our young people working with us, and it is one of the tragedies of our time that so many of them have become cynical about the accomplishments and prospects of science. I believe we can win many of them back, especially by showing them how effective we can be in working toward the solution of our environmental ills. We must prove to them that science and technology are among man's most creative and constructive forces—when they are used by creative and constructive men.

Finally, I think that in bringing together the many forces I have referred to tonight, and in emphasizing the importance of their working together, we must establish the leadership and goals to direct and sustain their efforts. Never before has the world had such a desperate need for greatness, for inspiration, for a vision. The cynics today will tell us that any vision we would have now would be a delusion. But I cannot agree. I feel as it says in Proverbs: "Where there is no dream—the people perish." Let us create that dream then and work to achieve it—not only that man shall live but that mankind shall be born.

THE PATTERNS OF CHANGE

PROTEST—PAST AND PRESENT [1]

J. BRONOWSKI [2]

Henry Steele Commager said recently that "the crisis in the university today is a tribute to its importance." The university is, Professor Commager continued, "the center of ideas, the center of research, the center of criticism and protest." All three centers have been much in the news; and no one, save the hopelessly indifferent or theatrically frivolous has taken the information lightly.

Some of the most perceptive analyses of current dissent and protest in the colleges have come from the philosophers and scientists. Even when their views on the state of the institutions vary widely, they still seem to come directly and meaningfully to grips with the substantive issues: the sense of alienation, the systems of values, the ethical imperatives, the propriety and efficacy of the proposed correctives.

On June 2, 1969, Dr. J. Bronowski, world-renowned mathematician-scientist-humanist, gave a speech at a conference entitled "A Search for the Meaning of the Generation Gap" sponsored by the San Diego County Department of Education. Dr. Bronowski, a senior fellow and trustee of the Salk Institute for Biological Studies, examined, in his usual clear manner, the need for "a philosophical foundation for the ethics of democracy." And what he had in mind was an ethic "the young can believe in." The "agreed ethic" must rest "on a common culture, and a common culture must be expressed in what is taught in schools and universities." The need is for "a core curriculum for all students, whose parts truly represent the constituents of modern culture." He believed the essential parts of such a curriculum should be science, anthropology, and literature.

Many students of public address are of course familiar with Dr. Bronowski's writings. Among the pieces that should have a special place on the reading list are "A Moral for an Age of

[1] Address delivered at a meeting of the San Diego (California) County Department of Education on June 2, 1969. Reprinted from *The American Scholar*, Volume 38, Number 4, Autumn, 1969. Copyright © 1969 by the United Chapters of Phi Beta Kappa. By permission of the publishers and author.

[2] For biographical note, see Appendix.

Plenty," which appeared in the Adventures of the Mind series
in the *Saturday Evening Post* (November 12, 1960) ; "The Reach
of the Imagination" (*American Scholar,* Spring 1967) , and *Science
and Human Values* (Harper, 1956).

The title of this essay is meant as a reminder that protest
is not a new invention of the 1960s—and this whether we
think it a divine invention or a satanic one. On the contrary,
protest has always been the normal apparatus to initiate
change in human societies. Whenever we say of some historic
pioneer that he was *original,* we imply that he was at odds
with the traditional view of his time, and that he ultimately
persuaded others to his view by voicing his dissent.

This is most obvious in the sciences which, from Galileo
to Albert Einstein, have always had to question the established explanations and replace them by new ones. So one
reason for the growth of heterodoxy has no doubt been the
spread of scientific education. Yet the same march of innovation, the same process of dissent and challenge, is evident
in other intellectual fields: for example, in the arts and in
philosophy. It has been equally important in politics and
social reform; there could have been no American Revolution and no French Revolution without such unorthodox
men as Benjamin Franklin and Thomas Jefferson and
Voltaire.

Lest that remark be passed over lightly, I pause to recall
that I speak as an Englishman to what George III would
have called a parcel of rebels—that is, an audience of Americans. You are a republic today because your forefathers
were impatient of social wrongs, what they called "a long
train of abuses and usurpations," and revolted against them
in 1776. This country was made by political dissenters and,
even before that, by religious dissenters. Unlike most of
you, I am not a Christian either: so it is fair that I remind
you also that you would not be what you are if Christ had
submitted to the religious authority of his elders—or if
Luther had done so later. It is a sobering lesson in history
that millions of people who dislike the contemporary forms
of protest still call themselves *Protestants.*

Progress by dissent then is characteristic of human societies. It has been responsible for the growth and success
of democracy in the last four hundred years, and the decline
and failure of absolute forms of government. For the crucial
feature of democracy is not simply that the majority rules,
but that *the minority is free to persuade people* to come
over to its side and make a new majority. Of course, the
minority is abused at first—Socrates was, and so was Charles
Darwin. But the strength of democracy is that the dissident
minority is not silenced; on the contrary, it is the business
of the minority to convert the majority; and this is how a
democratic society invigorates and renews itself in change
as no totalitarian society can.

Finally, it is natural that all through history the protesters have belonged to the younger generation, and the
defenders of tradition have been the older men. This is one
reason why dissent has usually come from the centers of
learning, and has often begun as an intellectual movement
before it became a popular one. It was so, for example, in
the time of Erasmus, and again in the decades of ferment that
preceded the Russian Revolution. There are several new
factors that underline this tendency today to which I shall
point later.

We see in general that protest is the age-old instrument
for human progress. Yet when this has been said to link past
to present, it remains evident that there are also differences,
and that protest today has some features that are special and
contemporary.

One feature that is peculiar to America is that the movement of dissent here is greatly occupied with getting justice
and equality for racial minorities. I shall refer to this important aim again, but I shall not speak about it much, because I cannot do so at first hand. I am a newcomer to this
country; my experience is almost wholly in European universities; and I shall therefore concentrate on those aspects
of student dissent that American universities share with
European universities.

The striking and universal feature in the protest of the young all over the world is that *it is not doctrinal.* We have been used in the past to associate new movements with some specific dogma: with women's suffrage, or socialism, or land reform, or even national socialism. There are no such ideological cure-alls in the minds of students today. Certainly they dislike the existing organizations of government pressure and social conformity, and they want them replaced by something more egalitarian, more personal, less rigid and manipulating. But the very fact that the students' protest runs across the existing political boundaries, from Berkeley to Warsaw, and from Prague to Paris and London, shows that there is no ideology that they think will solve the problems of the world overnight. The young now do not expect to reform society by a ready-made program with the points numbered from 1 to 14.

In particular, it is wide of the mark to think that dissent in this country is inspired by communism. Most students now find that idea laughable: they consider communism in East Europe to be a mechanical and dictatorial system of state that is as repugnant to them as any other autocracy. Otherwise, why would the universities in Poland have made their remarkable protests in 1968? The Polish establishment called those demonstrations a capitalist plot, of course, and that makes a neat match to the fears of our establishment. But the students in Poland and Czechoslovakia are not rooting for capitalism, and the students in the West are not rooting for communism; they are united in *rejecting both establishments.*

It is easy to be scornful of all this, and to say that the students' lack of dogma is an impractical and romantic approach to changing the world. Indeed it is: the heroic pictures of Mao and Che Guevara on the walls of dormitories show that. It may even be called negative and, worse, a purely destructive approach. But these easy criticisms miss what is crucial in the outlook of the young now, and new. They are not merely criticizing the systems of state in which their elders live, either east or west of the Berlin wall. They are criticizing the *systems of values* by which their elders live everywhere.

So the students' protest is not doctrinal because it goes much deeper: it is concerned with ethics. In the past there was a simple difference between the generations, all the way from politics to sports: the old were usually in favor of the status quo and the young were usually in favor of change. But simple differences like these, simple labels like conservative and liberal, will no longer do now. Now the difference between the generations is a total difference in posture—a rejection by each of the norms by which the other lives.

The generation gap is now a moral chasm, across which the young stare at their elders with distrust, convinced that the values that make for success are fakes. Evidently the first field in which young people are struck by this suspicion is public life, and there the undeclared war in Vietnam has had a disastrous impact. Who indeed could have believed that, twenty-five years after Pearl Harbor, national policy would be carried on like this?

Young people would like to be proud of their own nation (that, after all, is what the students from the minorities exemplify) and they were shocked to find that they could not be proud of the policy of America and her allies in Asia. This was coupled with a second shock, when they found that they could not be proud of the weapons and methods with which the war was waged.

But the greatest shock of all to the idealism of the young is the way in which official spokesmen manipulate and even hoodwink the public opinion that they are supposed to lead. A whole apparatus of evasion has been developed in which nothing is an outright lie, and yet nothing quite means what it seems to say. The very words are unreal: deescalation, ultimate deterrent, agonizing reappraisal—a tasteless vocabulary of plastic which George Orwell prophetically called Newspeak.

Plainly this language is not designed to *state* a policy but to *sell* it, and accordingly it is tailored to each audience in turn: the patriots here, the realists there, and the credulous everywhere. No wonder that students on both sides of the iron curtain think that politics is a career for actors rather than principals. This state of affairs has become so notorious in some countries that it has been christened with a euphemism all its own: it is called the credibility gap. That politely evasive phrase describes what is the fundamental outrage to democracy, namely, the concealment of knowledge; and more than anything else (I believe) this has been responsible for sapping the trust of the young in public standards.

It would be comforting if we could stop there and say, yes, some men in high places have disappointed the young, but after all they have their parents and teachers to look up to still. Unhappily, it is just here that the generation gap is different now from what it was thirty years ago. I can speak for this from my own experience, and I will do so.

I was brought up in Europe in an Orthodox Jewish household. My father was a devout believer, who was meticulous to the point of obsession in the practice of every detail of his religious faith. By the time that I went to college I no longer shared his beliefs, which seemed to me an anachronism. But I did not doubt for a moment that my father was sincere in what he believed and practiced. No one, not even the mutinous son that I was, could have thought my father a hypocrite. And as I respected him, so he respected me—in spite of my skepticism. My father thought me a hothead, but he did not doubt that I was sincere, too.

Today the generation gap cleaves through families and colleges, and there is little respect left in it. I need not trouble to spell out for you what the fathers think—and worse still, the grandfathers: they are the ones who write to the papers with such venom every day. Yet I must not quite neglect the phenomenon of those letters to the newspapers. Here we are in the country that prizes education more than any other country in the world; and in that country, here we are in the state of California, which prizes education more than any other state. And yet exactly here the correspondence columns are filled with such hatred against the young, such hysterical fear of change, that one cannot imagine how the writers picture a university. Do they expect education to run backward? Do they think that there can be progress without originality, and originality without dissent? Or would they really like to burn heretics?

Perhaps senior citizens always felt like this, and their grandsons paid no attention. But now the same gap has opened between fathers and sons. Whatever the generation, the sons no longer believe that the standards by which their elders judge them are genuine; on the contrary, they strike them for the most part as bald hypocrisy. I knew that my father lived by the precepts that he tried to impose on me. But most students today are convinced that their parents and teachers deceive themselves, and profess a traditional set of principles without even being aware that they do not live by them. In the eyes of the children, the generation gap now is a hypocrisy gap.

If those whom the young stigmatize were all reactionaries and anti-intellectuals, it would be easy to concur. Unfortunately, things are not so simple. A whole generation of liberals and humanists, to which I belong, is bewildered at the discovery that the young include us in their charge of hypocrisy. We made liberalism respectable by our labors, and turned it into an intellectual faith; and now we are distressed to find that our heroic memories of the hungry thirties and the Spanish Civil War are dismissed as an out-of-date mythology.

The fact is that we, the generation of intellectuals, have been a success, and our liberal and even radical ideas have not stood in our way on the road to affluence. And the young are suspicious of affluence: they do not believe that success comes so cheap to those who hold their principles dear. Success is a commodity sold on television in shatterproof bottles at bargain prices, and the children are no longer impressed

by those trappings of authenticity. They know in their hearts
that the successful man is a prisoner of the status quo, whatever high principles he may avow in the family circle or on
the rostrum.

When the French historian La Popelinière died in obscurity in 1608, his biographer wrote that he had died "of
a disease common to men of learning and virtue, that is, of
misery and of want." But that was in the past. Now men of
learning fare much better, and their sons and students are
correspondingly less certain of their virtue.

So it is not to be wondered that the young are restive
when they hear us pay lip service to intellectual truth. For
in the thirty years in which we have preached that, the world
has changed, and we have somehow forgotten to find new
foundations for the old truths. The economic exploitation
and social inequality of thirty years ago have been transformed since then, and will no longer do as grounds for the
human and liberal morality in which we still believe—and
believe rightly. As intellectuals, we have done little to formulate afresh *an ethic of liberalism on foundations that are
modern* and valid now. In my view, this is the central criticism that can be directed against intellectuals today, in and
out of the universities.

Here I must pause in my argument to say something
about the practical discontents in the universities. For, of
course, there are direct and practical causes that turn the
moral scruples of students into the bitter hand-to-hand
clashes with campus authority. Three causes are specifically
modern, and illustrate how education now differs from the
past—even the past of thirty years ago.

First, there are vastly more students now than there have
ever been before. There are about seven million students in
America at this moment, which is more than went to college
in the whole world in all the hundred years of the last century. What students in these numbers want from university
education must be different in kind from the academic programs of the past. So we are now engaged by necessity in the

experiment of finding a core curriculum and a culture to embody the aspirations of mass democracy. This is the cardinal problem to which I shall come back at the end of this essay. The demands of the minority groups for higher education are one part of the problem we have to solve. But the problem is the same for the majority, and is worldwide: what is the central content of contemporary knowledge that every young man and woman (and not just a few) ought to have in order to feel and act as educated citizens?

Second, young people now become physically and emotionally mature almost two years earlier than they did in the past. Yet while the age of biological maturity has fallen steadily, the age of university education has remained almost unchanged. As a result, the campuses are now peopled by grown men and women, yet are governed by traditions of organization and discipline that were made for adolescents. No wonder that the parents who remember themselves as striplings at college are outraged by the beards and the bosoms that they see there now—and by the intransigence that is natural in the bearded and the bosomed, especially when they have to be treated as children. The university system as it is, historically, is two years out of step with the attitudes and emotions of contemporary students, and is only suited to the young who are now in high school.

And third, the trouble on campus is a microcosm that reflects the troubles of administration and organization that dog any mass democracy. I have already said that democracy is a very special philosophy. It expresses the mind of the majority, yet it gives the minority the right to try to change the mind of the majority. That is, democracy is an instrument for change and progress.

But to make that philosophy work, democracy has to have an administration that is receptive to change. It has to be sensitive to what people want *before* they break the rules. And this is where organizations of state and government are failing us, and where most seriously the campus administrations are failing the students. I have been an administrator myself and I know the temptations. There is always some piece of business in the office that seems more urgent than the complaints of people. So the awkward issues are postponed; the grievances accumulate; and we stumble from crisis to crisis, never acting until the strike notices have been posted and people's blood is up. We never tackle a frontier dispute until there is shooting; a labor demand until the garbage is piled high in the streets; and the restlessness of the young until they invade the president's office.

The trouble on campus has a tremendous message: that we must discover how to run mass democracy so that things are changed *before* people get mad. In an age of technology, of constant practical change, this is a practical message to shake the world. Because if we do not get this right, then the process of peaceful change will break down, and people will turn to violence and minority rule everywhere. The trouble on campus is a storm signal to warn us that the philosophy of democracy will only survive if we reform the *practice* of democracy.

Yet when these practical things have been said, the intellectual problem comes back to meet us. We need to find a philosophical foundation for the ethics of democracy that the young can believe in. What divides democracy from its enemies is not a dogmatic distinction as between good and bad, your faith and mine, but is the basic distinction between tolerance and fanaticism—between persuasion and violence. When the students turn to disruption and hooliganism they show that our generation has failed to make the liberal values real to them. Instead we have demonstrated to them in a dozen political precedents, all the way from Ireland to Israel, that only men with guns get their demands. And calling out the National Guard will only reinforce that ugly lesson.

The young are looking for a universal ethic now as much as in the past, and here as much as in Czechoslovakia. If they strike you as amoral, look again: they are in search of a morality that shall be idealistic and realistic at the same time.

And if we think we have it in humanism, we shall have to find modern foundations for that.

It is pointless to exhort students to law and order, and to lecture them about rights and duties, in the absence of any foundation for human respect—and worse, in an atmosphere of cynicism that claims that human nature is a caged beast. Law and order are not ends in themselves; they are the means that society has invented to preserve justice, which is the harmony between individual freedom and communal need. Since only man among the animals is both individual and social, he has constantly to recreate the balance between these two sides of his nature. What we have to ask then of people, young and old alike, is not blankly that they respect the law, but that they respect every man as a man (whatever his opinions or his social function). And to bring that about, we have to make a modern analysis of the nature of man, derived from the natural and social sciences and equally from its expression in the arts. Only so shall we establish for everyone that the identity of man demands respect as an essential and, as it were, an existential condition of his being.

This is in a sense an academic program, and none the worse for that; and the universities are to be blamed for failing to attempt it. In a time of bold technical progress and of brilliant scientific discovery, one might have expected that humanists in the universities would also be eager to move into new fields, and that the study of the ethical nature of man would be most attractive to them. After all, many of the protesting students are suspicious of science and disillusioned by it, and are ready to look to the humanities for a lead. But in fact the departments of humanities have done little to move away from their traditional studies and toward the ethical content of their own subject matter. And yet that is surely what the arts can teach: the sense of identity with the inner lives of all men.

It is particularly sad that philosophy has remained remote from any genuine inquiry into the human mind and the dilemmas of personality. At a time when young men hunger for principles to guide their lives, philosophy has been preoccupied with forms of analysis in which, it rightly assures them, there surely are none to be found. So for thirty years now no philosopher has commanded, or has aspired to, that combination of intellectual and moral respect which made Bertrand Russell a giant in his generation.

I believe that there are principles to be found today to guide human conduct, as there were in the past. Today they must come out of modern knowledge of what makes us the creatures that we are, specifically human. We do not know the whole answer to that, of course, and no doubt we never will; but we know more than we ever did in the past. And what we know is not exclusively in science, and not exclusively in the humanities, but is a combination of both in which each illuminates the other. Only in this way, by understanding as exactly and as sympathetically as we can what men are, can we make the generations (past and present) agree to try to be what men should be.

In my view, this is a very practical task: for an agreed ethic must be based on a common culture, and a common culture must be expressed in what is taught in schools and universities. The great need, the great experiment in education now is therefore to put together a core curriculum for all students, whose parts truly represent the constituents of modern culture. I think there should be three parts: science, anthropology (as representative of social study) and literature.

In science, students need in the first place to learn enough physics, chemistry and mathematics (including some statistics) to make a foundation for biology in its contemporary form. As soon as they have the foundation, they should go on to biology as the central science in the core curriculum. The accent in biology should be on evolution: the evolution of life, of molecular structures and processes, of organs, of species and their behavior, and in the end, of man. The purpose should be to build up a picture of man as he is by nature, within the order of nature: what I have called elsewhere "an understanding of the evolution and the place of man" as a single conception. I will go on to quote what I said there:

He is, like the other primates, noisy, inquisitive, cooperative, intelligent, skillful, thoughtful, and as busy with himself as with his environment. These features are not common in the rest of the animal world, singly or in combination. They have been a great deal more important in the evolution of the primates than the territorial imperative and the aggressive drives which we share with other animals. And in the remarkable order of primates, the evolution of man is most remarkable and spectacular. His gifts of discrimination and judgment, the ability to speak, to remember, to foresee, to imagine and to think symbolically, his carriage and the freedom that it gives to hands and face, his face-to-face relations and his way of making love, his family life and the intimacy of his social values, are an incomparable biological equipment. They have evolved him, and in turn have been evolved by his own progress, within at most a few million years. From them he has his creative skill and his imaginative breadth of outlook, in which are intertwined his need for the society of others and his urge to think for himself.

As the second leg in what I will call my tripos curriculum, I have chosen anthropology. I prefer it to other branches of social study in a core curriculum, because I think students should not be preoccupied only with the forms of social institutions (including government) but should unravel the underlying beliefs and values that those express. Anthropology is the best discipline for the study of values, not as arbitrary social norms, but as expressions of human aims. In this sense, it carries on the scientific purpose of my first leg, and I can go on with my quotation:

It goes without saying that the picture of man that science presents to a bewildered and downcast public must be truthful. But that does not mean that it turns him either into a beast or into a computer. On the contrary, what makes the biological machinery of man so powerful is that it modifies his actions through his imagination: it makes him able to symbolize, to project himself into the consequences of his acts, to conceptualize his plans, and to weigh them one against another as a system of values. We are the creatures who have to create values in order to elucidate our own conduct and to learn from it so that we can direct it into the future.

For the third leg of my tripos I propose literature as the most accessible representative of the arts. The arts are important in the curriculum because they *express* the human condition directly, and as powerfully as the sciences *expound* it. Literature in particular should give the student a sense of the immediacy of human problems, an open door into the minds and passions of men, within which he finds himself to be both singular and universal. The gift of imagination makes man able to live his own life and a thousand others, and to draw from that network of experience a central concept of himself that can be a better guide to conduct than any book of moral precepts. Since I have presented these views in *The Identity of Man* I need not argue them here; I think they leave no doubt that literature can be as important a constituent in founding a modern ethic as can the sciences of biology and anthropology.

The need for a modern ethic of this kind, securely founded, is patent: because precisely the lack of it has turned the movements of protest toward self-righteousness and violence. Otherwise we are simply on the way to confronting dogma with dogma, force with ferocity, my right with your wrong. But these do not constitute the real division in human conduct. The fundamental distinction is between liberal and bigot, and at bottom it is the distinction between human and inhuman At the base of any educational reform, this is the distinction for which we have to find a secure, contemporary, and universal foundation.

DECLARATION OF CONSCIENCE—
TWENTY YEARS LATER [3]

MARGARET CHASE SMITH [4]

In the history of oratory there are numerous echoes of ideas and moods. With appropriate variation and adjustment, the theme of Ralph Waldo Emerson's "American Scholar" recurs regularly. Countless speakers have memorialized the American heritage. Inaugural addresses traditionally play upon common subjects.

A recent example is fresh in memory. On June 1, 1970, on the floor of the United States Senate, Margaret Chase Smith of Maine uttered a second Declaration of Conscience—this one twenty years later to the day—on the state of the nation's intellectual and psychological health. In 1950 she struck out against the tactics of the late Senator Joseph McCarthy and the radical right. In 1970 she spoke out against both the radical dissidents and those who would silence them. "The excessiveness of overreactions on both sides is a clear and present danger to American democracy." She warned that "the excesses of dissent on the extreme left can result in repression of dissent"; and "excesses on the extreme right, such as those twenty years ago, can mute our national conscience." "Every present sign," commented the New York *Times* editorially, "makes it plain that she is right. . . . We wish only that she had added some notice of the many young Americans today who do know and appreciate what she is talking about and who are working in increasing numbers within the political system to promote their views on the great issues of the day."

Mrs. Smith has spent thirty years in Congress—eight in the House of Representatives and twenty-two in the Senate. She is not given to the making of long speeches. Independent of spirit, and respectful of silence, she invariably bides her time in making decisions on major political matters. According to Warren Weaver of the New York *Times,* Mrs. Smith read the speech of June 1 from a handwritten text in large letters, with relatively few words on each sheet.

Twenty years ago on this June 1 date at this same desk I spoke about the then serious national condition with a

[3] Speech delivered on the floor of the United States Senate, June 1, 1970. Text furnished by Senator Smith, with permission for this reprint.

[4] For biographical note, see Appendix.

133

statement known as the "Declaration of Conscience." We had a national sickness then from which we recovered. We have a national sickness now from which I pray we will recover.

I would like to recall portions of that statement today because they have application now twenty years later.

I said of the then national condition, "It is a national feeling of fear and frustration that could result in national suicide and the end of everything that we Americans hold dear." Surely that is the situation today.

I said then, "I speak as briefly as possible because too much harm has already been done with irresponsible words of bitterness and selfish political opportunism." That is not only the situation today, but it is even worse for irresponsible words have exploded into trespass, violence, arson and killings.

I said then, "I think that it is high time for the United States Senate and its members to do some soul searching— for us to weigh our consciences—on the manner in which we are performing our duty to the people of the United States—on the manner in which we are using or abusing our individual powers and privileges."

That applies today. But I would add this to it—expanded application to the people themselves, whether they be students or construction workers, whether they be on or off campus.

I said then, "Those of us who shout the loudest about Americanism in making character assassinations are all too frequently those who, by our own words and acts, ignore some of the basic principles of Americanism—

The right to criticize;
The right to hold unpopular beliefs;
The right to protest;
The right to independent thought."

That applies today—and it includes the right to dissent against the dissenters.

I said then, "The American people are sick and tired of being afraid to speak their minds lest they be politically smeared. . . . Freedom of speech is not what it used to be in America. It has been so abused by some that it is not exercised by others."

That applies today to both sides. It is typified by the girl student at Colby College who wrote me, "I am striking with my heart against the fighting in Cambodia but I am intimidated by those who scream protests and clench their fists and cannot listen to people who oppose their views."

I said then, "Today our country is being psychologically divided by the confusion and the suspicions that are bred in the United States Senate to spread like cancerous tentacles of 'know-nothing, suspect everything' attitudes."

That applies today—but it must be expanded to the people themselves. Twenty years ago it was the anti-intellectuals who were most guilty of "know-nothing" attitudes. Today too many of the militant intellectuals are equally as guilty of "hear-nothing" attitudes of refusing to listen while demanding communication.

I said then, "I don't like the way the Senate has been made a rendezvous for vilification, for selfish political gain at the sacrifice of individual reputations and national unity."

That applies today. But I would add that equally I don't like the way the campus has been made a rendezvous for obscenity, for trespass, for violence, for arson, and for killing.

I said then, "I am not proud of the way we smear outsiders from the floor of the Senate and hide behind the cloak of congressional immunity and still place ourselves beyond criticism on the floor of the Senate."

Today I would add to that—I am not proud of the way in which too many militants resort to the illegalities of trespass, violence, and arson and, in doing so, claim for themselves a special immunity from the law with the allegation that such acts are justified because they have a political connotation with a professed cause.

I said then, "As a United States Senator, I am not proud of the way in which the Senate has been made a publicity platform for irresponsible sensationalism."

Today I would add that I am not proud of the way in which our national television networks and campuses have been made publicity platforms for irresponsible sensationalism—nor am I proud of the countercriticism against the networks and the campuses that has gone beyond the bounds of reasonableness and propriety and fanned, instead of drenching, the fires of division.

I have admired much of the candid and justified defense of our Government in reply to the news media and the militant dissenters—but some of the defense has been too extreme and unfair and too repetitive and thus impaired the effectiveness of the previous admirable and justified defense.

I said twenty years ago, "As an American, I am shocked at the way Republicans and Democrats alike are playing directly into the Communist design of 'confuse, divide and conquer.'" Today I am shocked at the way too many Americans are so doing.

I spoke as I did twenty years ago because of what I considered to be the great threat from the radical right—the threat of a Government of repression.

I speak today because of what I consider to be the great threat from the radical left that advocates and practices violence and defiance of the law—again, the threat of the ultimate result of a reaction of repression.

The President denies that we are in a revolution. There are many who would disagree with such appraisal. Anarchy may seem nearer to many of us than it really is.

But of one thing I am sure. The excessiveness of overreactions on both sides is a clear and present danger to American democracy.

That danger is ultimately from the political right even though it is initially spawned by the antidemocratic arrogance and nihilism from the political extreme left.

Extremism bent upon polarization of our people is increasingly forcing upon the American people the narrow choice between anarchy and repression.

And make no mistake about it, if that narrow choice has to be made, the American people, even if with reluctance and misgiving, will choose repression.

For an overwhelming majority of Americans believe that:

Trespass is tresspass—whether on the campus or off.
Violence is violence—whether on the campus or off.
Arson is arson—whether on the campus or off.
Killing is killing—whether on the campus or off.

The campus cannot degenerate into a privileged sanctuary for obscenity, trespass, violence, arson and killing with special immunity for participants in such acts.

Criminal acts, active or by negligence, cannot be condoned or excused because of panic, whether the offender be a policeman, a national guardsman, a student, or one of us in this legislative body.

Ironically, the excesses of dissent on the extreme left can result in repression of dissent. For repression is preferable to anarchy and nihilism to most Americans.

Yet, excesses on the extreme right, such as those twenty years ago, can mute our national conscience.

As was the case twenty years ago when the Senate was silenced and politically intimidated by one of its members, so today many Americans are intimidated and made mute by the emotional violence of the extreme left. Constructive discussion on the subject is becoming increasingly difficult of attainment.

It is time that the great center of our people, those who reject the violence and unreasonableness of both the extreme right and the extreme left, searched their consciences, mustered their moral and physical courage, shed their intimidated silence, and declared their consciences.

It is time that with dignity, firmness and friendliness, they reason with, rather than capitulate to, the extremists on both sides—at all levels—and caution that their patience ends at the border of violence and anarchy that threatens our American democracy.

A REQUIEM FOR JOE COLLEGE [5]

WILLIAM J. McGILL [6]

In an address before the National Conference on Higher Education in Chicago on March 3, 1970, Senator Mark O. Hatfield of Oregon remarked that of late "students are reacting to students, faculty, curriculum, administration, minority rights, our nation's inequities. The public is reacting negatively to this reaction. And the politicians are reacting to the public's reaction. No one gains in this vicious circle and everybody is hurt." This appears to be a clear summons to a new kind of educational leadership for a new day.

The colleges and universities continued in 1969-1970 to share the headlines with the Vietnam war. Ferment, bitterness, confrontation, and occasional disorder attracted public notice. Tragedy struck on several campuses. It was scarcely a good year for higher education. On the other hand, some important gains were registered. Needed institutional reforms and innovations were initiated or completed in many colleges. Massive demonstrations for causes held dear by many students underscored the idealism and public concern of American youth.

The speech reprinted here provides an impression of the new college. It was delivered before a meeting of the Acoustical Society of America in San Diego, California, on November 5, 1969. The speaker was William J. McGill, then chancellor of the University of California, San Diego. He has since been named to the presidency of Columbia University.

A native New Yorker, and former chairman of the psychology department at Columbia, Dr. McGill believes in what he calls "visibility of the administrator" during critical moments on the campus. In an interview reported in the New York *Times,* he said "it is absolutely essential that [the administrator] get out of his office and let students see him both as a person and a chancellor— to engage in active debate, to show both the humanity and strength that ought to go with leadership."

Said the reporter of Dr. McGill's workouts on the volleyball court: "He has faced many determined students across the net, and

[5] Address delivered at a meeting of the Acoustical Society of America in San Diego, California, on November 5, 1969. Text furnished by Dr. McGill, with permission for this reprint.

[6] For biographical note, see Appendix.

sometimes won." In these times, that would also be a laudable record across the administrative desk.

Joe College is dead. The era of reversible topcoats, pork-pie hats, yellow chrysanthemums and football weekends is now just a memory. We have pressed them all between the pages of time alongside our lost youth, and our bright hopes.

College life when I enrolled at Fordham University in 1939 organized itself around weekend spectaculars—football games and fraternity dances in the autumn, pilgrimages to nearby girls' colleges for "mixers" in the winter, and dates downtown in New York during the spring. It is a sweet-sad exercise to think back on those days.

I recall very little of my courses at Fordham except for a remembered sense of frustration over the inarticulateness of certain professors and the pomposity of others. Only one man, a Jesuit philosopher, Father Joe Murphy, ever tried to make me think. For the most part the classes and the professors were dreary, yet I experienced no acute feelings of protest. There was in fact muted relief that if the world outside was this easy, I would surely get ahead. Most of the memories of college that now remain are faces of girls without names, and chaotic glimpses of crowds of people outside stadiums or on dance floors. I can close my eyes and see through time to the red and gold decor of the Cafe Rouge of the old Hotel Pennsylvania. Glenn Miller is playing on the bandstand and my college friend Frank McIntyre sits across the table from me with his date looking almost Japanese in her effort to convey sophisticated composure. McIntyre played guard for Fordham and was one of my heroes. I lost track of him eighteen years ago.

Memories, of course, have a way of softening the brittle edges of youthful feelings. Most of the desperate struggle for identity, the despair, and the intense feeling beyond expression are etched away, leaving only the soft lights and sweet music. But the acuteness of my recall leaves no doubt that Joe College once lived, and every waking moment now tells me that he is dead. In fact, very little of Joe College remained when I left Fordham in 1943. We were at war. Life and death were very near at hand, and the antics of Joe College seemed rather unreal in comparison with tanks and bombers. Most of us, however, expected to see him return after the War, and perhaps he did for a while, but he is certainly gone now.

The college scene today is so different from Joe College as almost to defy comparison. There are still vestigial remains of the big game weekends but the spirit is manufactured. It is pure Madison Avenue rather than honest feeling. Television has made football games into a form of stagecraft and we are all more aware of being transmitted over the networks than of tough struggles out on the field. Even the officials look to the TV director before blowing their whistles.

Football and fraternity dances no longer occupy center stage on university campuses. Now we are alive with political concern, and a remarkable change in temporal sequencing has replaced the weekend spectaculars. Weekends now are quiet but ordinary weekdays display intense activity rising to a peak at the noon hour in the free-speech area.

In 1939 the campus folk heroes were the football team. At Fordham they were recruited from the coal mining communities of Pennsylvania. Largely by their own choice they led isolated existences, eating and sleeping together, mixing only rarely with the life of the college. We admired them but we did not really understand them or share their joys and sorrows.

In 1969 the folk heroes on campus are the minority students. They are recruited from the city ghettos. By their own choice they lead an isolated existence, eating and sleeping together and mixing only rarely with the life of the college. We admire them but we do not understand them. They do not permit us to share their sorrows or joys. They tell us we are unequipped to feel what they feel.

In 1939 we dressed and acted as junior members of the establishment we all admired. Soft tweed jackets and striped ties were the mark of the college man. The effect was so profound that I still wear them thirty years later, and nothing else feels comfortable. In 1969 the new generation of students feels despair over the colorless and comfortable surroundings that produced them. College boys now wear rough blue workshirts, blue jeans and heavy shoes. Their hair is long and often they cultivate a walrus mustache. Sometimes they favor a faded brown military tunic and a beret. McIntyre's girlfriend with her creamy face and blank sophisticated gaze is succeeded in 1969 by sad-faced girls with long Mona Lisa hair, wearing blankets and sandals; no makeup at all and all the pain in the world visible in their so-serious eyes. These boys and girls speak a rough peasant vernacular. Their feelings of rejection drive them to dress, speak and feel in kinship with oppressed workers, the children of the earth that their soft hands and easy lives can never approach in reality. Of course it is a game, a pose. But then so were the creamy-faced girls with Japanese composure and the tweedy boys smoking their pipes in 1939. We are all engaged in masks and symbolism telling those who view us what we wish to say about ourselves. It is only that in thirty years the masks have changed, and many of us now prefer to forget that student styles convey messages fraught with deep personal meaning.

In 1939 the campus spectaculars were sports events. In 1969 they are protest demonstrations. Then students displayed naïve excitement. Now we find overt moralistic anger. Then as now the idealism of youth filled the campus. Cynics and revolutionaries in small numbers sought to attack this idealism or to shape it to their ends, but the overriding sense of idealism prevailed. It is the same now. Some things about young people never change.

The chief difference between 1939 and 1969 is the extraordinary political sensitivity of the modern university campus. We lived then in the Nazi era. There was intense political concern but somehow it managed to intrude into our lives on campus only by taking our friends away unreasonably and unexpectedly. Now at noon the free-speech area boils with political ferment. Far-out groups hawk their far-out literature. A young faculty radical harangues a small crowd whipping up Pavlovian anger via references to black students shot in the back at Orangeburg, peaceful demonstrators brutally attacked by Mayor Daley's cops in Chicago, and a helicopter spraying gas over defenseless students on the Berkeley campus. The crowd grows. Shouts, obscene cries, and clenched fists vent suddenly angry feelings. Then the speaker delivers the punch in his message. "A brutal, oppressive administration—we have demands—nonnegotiable—march on the chancellor's office—NOW!"

An atmosphere of menace is quickly generated. College deans gather on the periphery of the crowd to warn and contain. The provost reaches for his telephone to call in his warning. "They are coming." Then a student jumps on the platform and aims darts of irony at the previous speaker. "He is trying to make the cafeteria food service sound like defoliation in Vietnam. The problem is the cafeteria, not the chancellor, and it is here at UCSD, not in Vietnam. How silly can you be?" There is a smattering of applause. Student listeners begin to drift away. The radicals move off to one side and plan for another day, deans relax, and the provost calls in "all clear."

A sense of barely contained anger is everywhere on the modern university campus. On almost any day, out of almost any cause, a storm may blow up. It feeds on the anger and expands so rapidly that the direction and scope of the difficulty is impossible to predict. Modern university administrations are geared to respond quickly to angry storms. Administrative tactics are aimed at dealing with the anger and wearing down the demonstrators. Anger tends to melt under the stress of continuous planning and meeting. Discussion groups of all sorts are proposed. No one on campus can oppose discussion of any issue. The radical leaders are identified, and baited by faculty and administrators with experience at taking on the radicals in open debate. They know where all the soft spots are. "I understand, professor, that you urged the students to strike today but nevertheless met your own class. Are you afraid you might miss a pay check? The rest of you understand that he is trying to use you, don't you?" And so it goes.

In the midst of all this political sensitivity and angry fermentation, there is little on the modern campus to remind us of the days when Joe College held sway. The ferment and the anger make for a wholly new campus ambience totally removed from the experience of listeners past the age of forty. Where does it come from and what does it all mean as seen by university people experienced in working with these new problems?

First, nothing is more obvious to us than the reality of student anger. The phenomenon extends to many junior faculty members and graduate students. Anger is directed at the war in Vietnam, racism, poverty and exploitation in our cities, and the evils of a faceless society. But in a larger sense this anger is a reflection of problems more closely related to the current educational milieu. Student unrest flourishes in France where there is no Vietnamese agony and no racial conflict. Anger and destructiveness is at its peak in the universities of Japan where polite discourse is an art unmatched in refinement anywhere in the world. Unrest boils among students in nearly all the major industrial nations of the world; the United States of America, England, France, West Germany, Italy, Czechoslovakia, Poland, Russia, China, Japan. In each instance there is an advanced technology which must be served by the educational system. Where that technology is skyrocketing as it is in this country and in West Germany and Japan, student problems are especially acute.

Technical and scientific advances have produced an enormous growth of knowledge in a relatively short time. The scientific literature, for example, doubles every decade. New fields develop rapidly, new technical skills are demanded and old knowledge is made obsolete slowly. It is worth remembering that computer technology, solid state physics, and molecular biology were virtually nonexistent before World War II. Such extraordinary changes generate immense strains on college and university curricula. The latter are not reformed annually despite what the catalog and the public relations officers say. Instead, new requirements are piled upon old ones and education becomes stretched out in the process. In 1970 a Ph.D. will simply not provide enough training for serious students in the basic sciences, the health sciences, or even in social science. Two to five years of post-doctoral study will be required beyond the Ph.D. Students entering upon these professions, or the occupations served by them, must be prepared to postpone basic decisions about their lives, to delay commitments to a home and family in most instances until they are past thirty years of age. Moreover, the time spent in apprenticeship is continuing to stretch out alarmingly as the technology continues to grow.

We find ourselves faced increasingly with an archaic degree structure and with patchwork curricula desperately in need of reform. The sheer weight of modern education places extreme demands on students, alienating them in increasing numbers. There is no time in a modern college for the development of a personal philosophy or for dealing with the moral questions posed by society. Students find themselves in a rat race for grades with the way barred for further development in the technical professions if they fail. The race starts almost from the day they step into class. They come to the university looking for a well-formed philosophy of life and for a way to confront basic questions. Instead they find complex variables, cell biochemistry, and competition for grades. Out on the plaza, in the free-speech area, the radicals discuss basic philosophy and moral questions.

Increasingly, students are turning to the philosophers, humanists and social scientists in their search for answers. The growth of enrollment in these areas during the past decade has been nothing less than phenomenal. It appears at the present time that one quarter to one third of our undergraduate student body has become alienated in varying degrees from the university and from the values of a middle-class society. The alienation seems to be growing year by year. These points provide an illuminating rationale for the growth of anger and rejection among university students. The strange dress, the need for intense communal feeling, the seeking after naturalistic simplicity are certainly more comprehensible if we suppose that such students are rejecting mass culture, and the relentless anonymity of a runaway technology.

The fault lies not in our students but in us. We educators have failed. It is not easy to imagine how we might have succeeded, but the mass of alienated students, misdirected, angry idealists furnish us daily reminders of the scope of our failures. Thus our problem is not the handful of destructive revolutionaries in our midst. It is the mass of alienated students so desperately eager to be raped if only the revolutionaries can develop an issue to attract them.

People's Park in Berkeley exemplifies this principle. It was conceived by a handful of closely knit Telegraph Avenue guerrillas who saw an opportunity to seize a piece of university property in proclaimed defiance of property rights, and yet to represent it as an effort by powerless street-people to add a touch of beauty to their lives. The device was clever and the university's options for tactical maneuver were severely limited by the climate of public anxiety in which it now operates. The importance of People's Park was not the revolutionary seizure of property, but the fact that subsequently this issue drew 7,000 students to the steps of the state capitol in Sacramento and 30,000 more to a Berkeley demonstration.

Administrators in the University of California have experienced too much anxiety and have been through too many confrontations to be thought of as cowardly or inexperienced. These administrators know the potential for disaster that lies in the progressive alienation of their student bodies. They seek maneuvering room in order to deal with local manifestations of the alienation, struggling to replace anger with reason. The reflective reader who demands order on university campuses should ask himself whether a gas-spraying helicopter increases or reduces tensions associated with outrage over injustice. Does it convince students that we are a reasonable, responsible society? This is not meant to be an apology for the student-led mob that attacked police at People's Park. No apology for such excesses is possible. My question is addressed to the proper modes of controlling such angry mob behavior when the control is exercised by a reasonable and responsible society.

University administrators now face such questions and make such decisions daily. If they seem to avoid taking the hard line that outraged citizens demand, it is because these administrators understand the scope and the force of the alienation process afflicting their student bodies in 1969. When they make their decisions cleverly, alienation is diminished, anger fades, and a measure of harmony prevails on campus. When administrators lack firmness, anger and demands spiral. Advocates of student power sense weakness and move in on it. Administrators taking a blind, hard line find that they quickly alienate their entire student body and the first serious issue generates an explosion.

Experienced college administrators in 1969 walk the narrow line between firmness and flexibility, listening to and watching the ambience, working to replace anger by reason. This administrator, at least, longs for the days of Joe College when problems were simpler and expectations were greater. The requiem for Joe College is sung daily at UCSD and the singing comes chiefly from the chancellor's office. But alas, Joe College is gone—gone with our youth, our dreams, and our naïve expectations. In this harsh world of 1969 we must draw our breath in pain.

DO NOT REFUSE US [7]

MARTHA J. SARA [8]

Over fifty thousand native citizens live in Alaska. They include Aleuts, Eskimos, and Indians, many of whom have grown restive in a society which denies them the cultural and economic advantages enjoyed by most majority groups. Accordingly, a young native leadership is gaining strength and recognition. The major "article of faith" for this leadership is getting congressional approval of its land claim—usually referred to as "Indian title," a right deriving from continuous use and occupation during many generations.

Perhaps the most influential organization for the promotion of the claims is the Alaska Federation of Natives (AFN). It has presented to Congress a plan for the settlement of the claims. Among the requests are (a) 40 million acres of land in the native areas and hunting grounds, (b) cash payment of $500 million for other lands claimed by virtue of aboriginal occupancy, and (c) a 2 per cent royalty on revenues from gas, oil, and other leasable properties in state and Federal areas of Alaska.

In a special report prepared by Howard W. Pollock, Representative at Large from Alaska, arguments pro and con on the land claims question are set forth. Among the arguments advanced by those who support the claim are:

> [The contention] that Imperial Russia did not own Alaska, that its traders and agents only barely touched and briefly occupied peripheral and isolated coastal areas of the great land, had never seen or subjugated most of the aboriginal inhabitants, and were in fact, as the Russian America Company, directed by the Russian government not to spread their rule from the coast where trapping and hunting were taking place, nor, to make any effort to conquer the tribes inhabiting the coasts. It is further advocated that the historical international law of right to possession, title, and sovereignty by conquest did not pertain so far as Alaska and its people were con-

[7] Speech presented on October 17, 1969, at hearings of the Subcommittee on Indian Affairs of the House Interior and Insular Affairs Committee. Text furnished by Miss Sara, with permission for this reprint.

[8] For biographical note, see Appendix.

cerned, that the simple planting of a national flag on the soil by a foreign intruder and exploiter would not secure the land of Alaska for that nation or any nation at no cost to it, and, accordingly, that the United States really bought stolen property from Russia.

The spokesmen for the natives assert that since the land of Alaska has never been wrested from the Indians, Eskimos, and Aleuts by any act of hostility or conquest by either imperial Russia or the United States, nor taken by a legislative act or judicial determination of abandonment on the part of the natives, the land continues to belong to them by reason of aboriginal and historic use and occupancy. Further, it is pointed out that Alaska was sold to the United States by the Russian government without consultation with the Indian, Eskimo or Aleut inhabitants, and at no time since then has there ever been any agreement by aboriginal natives to extinguish their ownership in the lands of Alaska. (A bill passed by the Senate in August 1970 contains certain aspects of this plan. But the New York *Times* remarked editorially that it was "too limited to be an act of national generosity and too narrowly conceived to be a social breakthrough.")

During mid-October 1969, the Subcommittee on Indian Affairs of the House Interior and Insular Affairs Committee conducted hearings in Fairbanks, Alaska, on the Native Claims question. One of the speakers on October 17 was Martha J. Sara, a young Eskimo undergraduate student at the University of Alaska. Her statement deserves a wide reading. Combining grace and dignity with compassionate appeal, it voices the fervent hope and aspiration of the young Alaska natives for a humane settlement of a practical request.

Mr. Chairman, members of the board, my name is Martha J. Sara. I'm an Eskimo. I was born and raised in Bethel. I'm a junior at the University of Alaska. My major is sociology and I plan to go on and become a social worker.

On behalf of the Theata Club, which is an organization of native students on the University of Alaska campus, and on behalf of myself, I would like to say that I'm grateful for the right and am happy to take the responsibility to testify on behalf of the Native Land Claims.

Along with hundreds of other native young adults, I've taken the responsibility of becoming educated to better equip myself for our coming responsibilities in the management of our own affairs.

This is not an easy undertaking.

Although I am not the best example available, I will use myself. After high school I entered a school of nursing in Los Angeles. It was difficult for me because I had to overcome handicaps not faced by most American youths. I entered a different culture. Along with the dynamic process of learning what the school offered, I also had to adjust to new values and surroundings. I graduated and became a registered nurse at the age of nineteen. I was filled with a sense of accomplishment and I applied for employment at the Public Health Service Hospital in Bethel. Never before had they employed an associate in arts degree registered nurse—and so young. They had to get permission from Washington; permission was granted. I worked only one year when our community decided to open a prenatal home in Bethel through the assistance of the Office of Economic Opportunity. A director was needed with the qualifications of a registered nurse. I enthusiastically wrote a letter of application even before applications were printed. I knew the people and a lot of the future clients having worked most of the year in the maternity ward in our hospital. To my delight I was hired. Complications arose, however, because someone pointed out that in order to be a director of a prenatal institution in the state of Alaska one had to be twenty-five years old, and I was not yet even twenty-one. Letters were written on my behalf and permission was granted from Juneau for me to keep and fill the position. The funding was unsure because the deadline for occupancy was nearing and the building was unfit for expectant mothers as far as the state sanitarian, state fire marshal, and child welfare institution directors were concerned. Complete renovation of the physical plant and procurement of necessary equipment was urgent. Needless to say, I became an amateur painter, plumber, carpenter, electrician, diplomat, beggar, and petty larcenist. Local men did the plumbing, carpentry, and electrical work in conjunction with the BIA. Local boys under the neighborhood youth program did the painting. Used furniture was procured from the hospital through GSA. Supplies were ordered and opening day saw us admitting our first lady! We struggled and worked for what we wanted and got it. Of course we had the assistance and backing of the agencies, but the native peoples involved made it work. We were competent and proved it.

I am here representing a body of eager, willing young adults ready to learn, work, and show our capability in the management of our own affairs. I am just one of many who are willing to struggle for an education, who are willing to work hard, the way we worked on the Bethel Prenatal Home.

We are not asking for all our land—just a portion of it and if you grant it to us, we will have to strive very hard because what we are asking for is less than what we believe is fair. But we are capable of striving very hard.

And how shall you refuse us? You who have centuries of learning, education, civilization, colonization, expansion, domination, exploitation behind you? How shall you refuse us?

Do not refuse us because we are young! In youth there is energy, drive, ambition, growth, and new ideas. Do not refuse us because we are young! For we shall mature!

Do not refuse us because we are undereducated! We are learning fast; and utilizing our newly gained knowledge, comparing and weighing the truths and benefits of this knowledge. We know that the 40 million acres we are asking for will provide a minimum protection to hunting and fishing. We understand that we need the identification with, and the feeling for our *own land*. We also realize that we need this land as an economic base for our people. The land will be used as a commodity in our economic base. We can accomplish this with 40 million acres. Five hundred million dollars is a lot of money. We understand what a vital role this can play in the economic base of our people. We realize that with proper and careful handling and investment of this money we can make it work for us. We do not plan to make improvements without first establishing a sound economic base which will provide for growth and return. After this is established, then we can begin our improvements. We will then be able to maintain and expand these improvements. We realize that we can not only benefit our people, but *all* of Alaska. All this for $500 million. Do not refuse us because we are still learning! For we are fast learning!

Do not refuse us the chance to progress! We too have a dream for the progress of our land. We hold a superior position to develop our country because it is our country, and we love it. We will be more cautious in its utilization—and I deliberately use the word "utilization" instead of "exploitation." We will weigh each prospect carefully to assure ourselves that we are making the best decision for our generation and those generations to come. We are not here to grab; we are here to live with the growth of our native land. Do not refuse us the chance for progress. For we too share the dream of progress.

Do not refuse us because you are afraid we don't have competent leaders! I represent a generation of paradoxes. We are paradoxes in the fact that we are the closest links to the parties farthest separated in this issue. One of these groups is our beloved elders whom we left back home only a short time ago, who, along with others, still cling to the old ways and depend upon the land for subsistence. Another group is made up of our able leaders, native and white, who are presently in positions of decision. We are close to the old ones and the people back home because, having recently left them, their problems, worries, and fears burn deep in our hearts. We know what makes them happy; we know what can fill them with contentment; we know what gives them hope. At the same time we are close to our leaders in the fact that we are striving and aspiring to their positions of decision. Native young people are rising up to meet the demands and expectations of a foreign and sometimes hostile society. The day of our leadership is not too far off. When that day of fulfillment comes, I would like to think that we can proudly take our places side by side with the present leaders to direct the affairs of our own people. In their wisdom they can quell our fears, channel our energy, help shape our innovative ideas, direct our aggression, and interpret our anxieties. Together we can provide able leadership! Do not refuse us for fear of poor leadership! For we are capable leaders.

Do not refuse us simply because you purchased the sovereign right of our land! Our fathers since time began have paid dearly for our homeland every generation. They struggled against the harshest environment known to man and survived to teach us to do the same. Each generation paved the way for the next. Do not refuse us because you purchased this right! For our forefathers paid for it long before your forefathers had the money.

Do not refuse us because we are a minority! For this is America! We have proved in many ways that, not only do we take advantage of our rights and freedoms along with other Americans, but we are willing to, and have, fought equally for all its privileges. Our native soldiers fought and died for the United States in World War II, the Korean War, and in the present war in Vietnam. As American citizens, we have equal rights and have taken on equal responsibility. So do not refuse us because we are a minority! For this is America!

In closing I would like to say that competence is something that has to be proven. And as young native adults we have demonstrated our abilities and are now proving it.

I would like to add that we are deeply grateful to you all for taking time out of your busy schedules to come and hear our testimonies. It is deeply appreciated. Thank you! Quyana cakneq!

A TIME FOR RECONSTRUCTION [9]

William M. Birenbaum [10]

Colleges and universities are deeply concerned about their institutional roles. How much of the traditional function of higher education should be preserved? What sort of accommodation should be made to the demands that colleges serve more fully the social needs and aspirations of the community? What type of orientation can and should be made to a rapidly developing urban society? How can minorities be brought more fully and meaningfully into the mainstream of educational experience? Should the administrators accede to the pressures for an active institutional participation in politics? Should the requirements for admission to colleges be relaxed, or done away with? How can the colleges help to improve the quality of American life? These are but a few of the questions affecting the expanded role which colleges and universities are expected to serve. Higher education is launching forth on a new mission.

Many proposals have been made recently to restructure the institutions so as to make them more responsive to the needs of the communities and the nation. In 1967, Clark Kerr, director of the Carnegie Study of Higher Education in America, suggested that urban-grant universities be established, modeled roughly upon the idea embodied in the Morrill Act of 1862. Just as the Morrill Act made public lands available for educational institutions promoting agricultural and mechanical arts, so the urban-grant concept would provide land and possibly buildings, at the expense of the Federal Government, for serving the special needs of the cities. Incidentally, this is already being done in a limited way through urban renewal projects.

Despite some criticism of the two-year community colleges, they have taken deep root in the educational system and may, in fact, become its most important unit. Over one thousand such institutions are currently in operation. They accommodate nearly two million students. In anticipation of a doubled enrollment during the decade, the Carnegie Commission on Higher Education

[9] Address delivered on the occasion of Mr. Birenbaum's inauguration as president of Staten Island Community College of the City University of New York, New York City, September 30, 1969. Text furnished by Mr. Birenbaum, with permission for this reprint.

[10] For biographical note, see Appendix.

proposed in its June report that from 230 to 280 additional community colleges be set up before 1980.

In the address below, William M. Birenbaum advanced another proposal for a new kind of college for an urban society. Speaking on the occasion of his inauguration as president of Staten Island Community College in New York on September 30, 1969, he expressed doubt that the two-year colleges could meet the educational needs of the cities. The time available for training the students is too short; the idea of college as a community cannot be developed. Accordingly, he proposed that the new institutions "be solidly based upon a new amalgamation of the resources of the high schools and the colleges"; stand "for real and total integration"; "take a realistic and humane view of time"; "be honest about the Establishment's prejudices regarding quality and credentials"; "reestablish the connection between thinking and acting"; and "recognize that although the older generations do have something they alone can convey to the younger, what the young may teach each other is at least as important."

The adoption of a policy for open admissions in the City University of New York by the fall of 1970 is one of the most significant decisions ever made in urban higher education. The Board of Higher Education's decision anticipates the most historic educational development in our country since the Morrill Act established land-grant colleges in 1862.

The last Congress, during the presidency of Lyndon B. Johnson, opened the door to an extraordinary opportunity for the present Administration. Section 508 of the Amendments to the Higher Education Act of 1968 provides:

On or before December 31, 1969, the President shall submit to the Congress proposals relative to the feasibility of making available a postsecondary education to all young Americans who qualify and seek it.

This provision now preoccupies planners in the Department of Health, Education, and Welfare, and undoubtedly will play a featured role in President Nixon's message to the next Congress. These events in Washington and in City University indicate that in these final decades of the twentieth century, the earth's most mature technological state will provide some form of universal education beyond the twelfth grade for all of its people.

Such an extension of educational opportunity will lead to the reconsideration of every institutional form of higher education, and to an intensive fresh look at the relationships between the universities and the industrial, technical, cultural and other nonacademic centers of learning in our society.

These new developments place the two-year colleges on an urgent new front line.

The two-year college is a unique American educational invention of the twentieth century. In 1900, there were but eight such schools enrolling fewer than a hundred students. This fall, more than a million young Americans are enrolled on almost a thousand community college campuses. Now, the Carnegie Corporation's Commission on Higher Education proposes, pursuant to the Comprehensive Community College Act of 1969, that five hundred new community colleges be built by 1976.

My question is: Can the two-year college meet the educational needs of America's cities today? I doubt it.

The junior college movement arose out of two very different lines of thought. One held that the first two years of the American undergraduate college were essentially comparable to the last two years of secondary education in the European systems, and that what we do with freshmen and sophomores in our colleges should not be done in a so-called *real* university. Seen as extensions of our high schools, the two-year colleges would keep the university itself *pure* within the terms of elitist European academic traditions.

But another position saw the two-year colleges as grand doorways through which Everyman would pass en route to his own realization of the American Dream. These were to be the people's colleges in the traditions of Thomas Jefferson, Horace Mann, and the Morrill Act, teaching those things the people needed and wanted to know to make a living, and to live as free men. They were meant to serve the communities where the people lived. They were meant to emphasize teaching, and to provide a post-high-school learning opportunity for large numbers of young Americans denied direct entry into the traditional colleges and universities.

Elements of both of these positions are reflected in what the community colleges have become. Nationally, about a third of the students who now enter them go on to the four-year colleges and the higher degrees. For these students the community college is indeed a doorway. But it also serves as a filter for the senior system, and to keep this door open— to remain a respectable filter—the two-year college must honor the curricular values and styles, often no longer viable, of those colleges which originally rejected their student clientele.

For the majority of its students, the community college provides a terminal "higher education," consisting usually of preparation for the middle-level industrial and technological economy. For these students the doorway may not be grand, but it *is* an opening.

Because the two-year colleges have welcomed large numbers of young Americans whom the traditional institutions in the first instance rejected, they now occupy a key position in the struggle for social justice and equality in urban America.

The two-year college movement came late to our great cities. Even today, the majority are located in the rural towns, suburbia, and the small cities not graced by a major university.

Recent academic upheavals in our great cities—events and ideas which have stormed and breached the austere walls of Columbia, City College and Harvard—put the antique prejudices about the community college in a somewhat different light. The basic idea of the community college was to assault and demolish those same walls which have kept out the oppressed, the downtrodden, and the exploited. Now, as the medieval idea of the university licks its wounds and picks up its pieces, there are some who would value the two-year college solely as a kind of low-cost educational pail with which they may bail themselves out of their badly leaking academic boats.

Through the growing ferment in our urban high schools and among the urban youth, spectacular and durable new creative forces have been released. Our young people are suspicious of our interpretation of history. They are impatient with "adult" hypocrisy. They are discontent with the way our power systems operate, the way we use the new technology, the way we estimate the new potential of the human spirit. By 1975, people under twenty-five will comprise the majority of our population. Those now in charge of the machinery of American society make a catastrophic miscalculation if they assume that the things which now plague us will somehow magically go away as the young grow up. After two centuries, America is younger than ever before, still growing up.

A typically American answer to many of the country's problems is simply to grow bigger. By doing more and more of the same, we have tragically magnified the causes of the discontent and the disruptions.

In the process of being made bigger, the educational system has been divided into increasingly separate and distinct ghettos which we call high schools, community colleges, senior or "regular" colleges, graduate and professional schools.

We have put each part on a separate physical island, segregating levels of learners from each other, students and faculties from each other, the younger and the older from each other, teaching and research from each other, constantly foreshortening the periods of time in which any particular group of teachers and students might associate with each other in a common learning endeavor. And around each geographic and temporal academic ghetto, we repair and fortify those walls which segregate campus from community, academic professional from nonacademic professional, and the act of learning to think from the rich urban opportunities for thoughtful action.

In the undergraduate structure, we segregate the senior system from the junior; and within the two-year campuses we segregate the vocationally directed students from those who are to enter the liberal arts stream.

Finally, the intentions and assumptions built into this system segregate American youth by class. Within the terms of the contemporary American city, this results ultimately in a segregation by life styles, economic status, cultural aspirations, and race.

Over a third of the inexcusably small minority group enrollment in the nation's universities is contained on the all-black southern campuses—and over half of the remainder, nationally, congeals in the two-year colleges. In our own city, this system has channeled the preponderance of the black and Puerto Rican enrollments into the community colleges and, until quite recently, into the terminal, vocationally aimed, technology programs within these community colleges.

We have assumed that poverty is exclusively an economic concept—that if we prepare young people for participation in the middle levels of the technological economy, we also educate and equip them for mobile participation in the larger American society. This assumption ignores what is going on in the heads of black youth. Their interests assume economic opportunity and extend beyond it in sharp new thrusts to the connections between knowledge and social justice, political power, and cultural identity. This assumption ignores what is going on in the heads of our brightest and most interesting middle-class white youth. Many of them, midst the consummate beauty of the moon walk, the maddening magnitude of the Vietnam venture, and the sustained prosperity of the nation, assume that our knowledge and our know-how can produce not only a comfortable way of life, but also a life style filled with new and deeper meanings, with goals, delights, and achievements, with a music

and an art and individual love relationships their parents
have not yet known. In our older wisdom we may think that
what the young assume now is too much—insane, unreal,
impractical. But given *where we* are and *how we* are, to
what lesser goals would we have them aspire?

During the half century or so that we have used the four
collegiate years, of nine months each, measured by the un-
changing and relentless credit-hour system, mankind has
enjoyed its most phenomenal knowledge growth. What we
are now trying to fit into this obsolete system just doesn't
fit any longer. It can't be done—not in a time of the atom,
the moon, TV, pot, the pill, the recognition of the black as
a human being, as well as the fantastic growth in more traditional subject-matter areas. We are trying to contain and
control the knowledge explosion and new human aspirations
in a fragile and sterile eggshell. We are trying to put
Humpty-Dumpty together again with bureaucratic pan-
aceas which ignore the incredible gap between what *we* may
know and the archaic institutional forms which we use to
help *people* know.

In the two-year colleges we have but sixty to seventy of
these credit hours—twenty to twenty-five one-semester courses
through which we can hope to do something with the state
of mind of those angry, upset, usually miseducated, previously rigidly processed, beautiful young people who come to us.
For most of these young people, we are supposed to reduce
six thousand years of recorded human experience to twenty
courses, more or less. For the majority of our students entering the vocational programs, we are lucky if we can reserve
a small fraction of this time—three to six courses—for the
salient liberating subjects such as history, the arts, literature,
philosophy or politics. Even in the technologies like electrical or civil engineering, nursing or the paramedical sciences, the knowledge required for future upward-bound performance in the job market now extends well beyond what
we can honestly convey in two nine-month years.

Consequently, with those students coming to us with high school diplomas reflecting the least success in a failing secondary system, the least prior education in the subjects vital to the conduct of free men—with these students we are doing the least. To these young Americans acutely concerned about social justice and being free, we respond with a narrow and incomplete and ultimately dishonest version of the beauty of knowledge, the sanctity of the opportunity to learn, the intricacy and delicacy of probing the human mind and heart.

Finally, we have tragically retreated from the idea of the college as a community at a time when one of the deepest longings in hearts of the young is for a community. These students have a passion to know people well in their own terms, to master the control of self, for a time and a place to bring impersonal bureaucracies and sterile geographies into human scale, for a situation to which a human can belong. One out of three New Yorkers changes his place of residence at least once every five years. The young urban American entering college now has had little enough opportunity to sink his roots down, face day-to-day the meaning of community, friendship, sustained and hard endeavor, of being around long enough to be held responsible for what he starts and does. He has virtually no time in which to make and correct an honest mistake, even as he sees our failure to correct our own mistakes.

In our two-year colleges, the students whom we ask to participate in campus government, to obey the laws and maintain the order, hardly have enough time to get their bearings, meet the faculty, make friends, and master the laws, before they are on their way out. We move students around like pawns on a chessboard through bits and pieces of academic time and campus space—from two-year college to four-year college, from college to graduate school, from technical center to liberal arts center.

How can we expect the young to learn in a lawful and orderly community climate, when we process them through systems subversive of learning, in places in which the law is often arbitrary and the order may be imposed? How can we prepare the young for the future in the great cities on campuses hostile to the city? How can we talk about a community of scholars under conditions which work against a community of anybody?

For the foreseeable future, our cities are the new settings for American democracy. Many of the medieval European traditions and early American rural values simply are not applicable to the situation we now are in. Urban America cries out for new institutional inventions, for a new approach to the content of our way of life. Our educational systems must be among the first to heed this cry, for they enjoy a priority in the means of producing those things now essential to physical survival and the new freedom.

This occasion today is, in a sense, a ceremonial fiction since I have in fact already served for a full year as president here. I have sought, during that year, to be careful not to leap to half-baked or rash conclusions.

But I am convinced, after those twelve months as president of Staten Island Community College, that the present two-year format of the community colleges is no longer viable in the city. Two years is just not long enough to accommodate the kind of education our students are demanding and ought to have. It is not long enough to convey all that we must convey, and to establish the sense of community which is so necessary in a teaching and learning situation.

I want today to propose a new kind of college for the communities in our cities.

First, the new institutions we invent to provide a universal educational opportunity beyond the twelfth grade must be solidly based upon a new amalgamation of the resources of the high schools and the colleges. It makes no sense for a secondary school system to educate more and more people who will require some formal educational experience beyond grade twelve, separate and apart from the activities of systems claiming jurisdiction beyond grade twelve. It makes no sense for the colleges to receive more and more students from the high schools into larger and larger remedial programs conceived and directed separate and apart from the talents of the secondary system. The Board of Education and the Board of Higher Education in New York should be the first in the nation to create an Institute for Universal Advanced Education through which may be pooled the faculties, the campuses, the laboratories, the student and faculty talents and the development of programs in the high schools and the colleges. There should be a common leadership, and a common purpose.

Second, we must launch new colleges for the communities of the city which stand for real and total integration—the integration of races, and of cultures, of classes, and of life styles, and most important of all, of bodies of knowledge bearing upon vocation with bodies of knowledge bearing upon what Americans must know, beyond making a living, in order to be free. Within the sphere of a united campus, we must bring the technologies together again with the liberal arts, the younger with the older students, the students with the teachers, the two-year degree with the four-year degree. Through the reunification of subject matter, space and time, we must consciously work to restore a sense and a reality of community in the learning endeavor. We must stop breaking things up, and begin to put things together again in the image of man.

Third, the new college for the urban community must take a realistic and humane view of time. It must perform within the scope of twelve-month calendar years. It must stop saying that its ultimate rewards—the degrees—will be apportioned according to the system's rigid view of time by the credit hours. Instead, it must regard the infinite variety of human styles, commitments and talents, and deliver its rewards in terms of the humans it serves. For some this may mean a year; for others, six or seven. The variable should be the person, not the scheme.

Fourth, the new community college must be honest about the Establishment's prejudices regarding quality and credentials. While the tests and criteria we now use to admit people —actually, to determine who shall be kept out—do apply with reasonable efficiency to those for whom they were designed, they tell us virtually nothing about the rest. We possess no testing instrument which reveals the real potential of the high school dropout, the potential of the urban poor, the urban oppressed, those whom American society has traditionally swept aside. At the present time, there is only one way—one, expensive way—to test their potential, and that is to offer them an honest chance. We must provide that chance, and shift our emphasis from an obsession with our version of the quality of those we do admit to an obsession with the quality of those we turn out. We should concentrate on the quality of those who finally get the degree, and relax a bit about quality standards at the beginning when we make the educational opportunity available.

Fifth, the new community college must reestablish the connection between thinking and acting. It must recognize, given the state of our knowledge and the wealth of nonacademic talent in the great city, that decision-making action is often the best context through which people learn. We are now beginning to acknowledge this fact in medical education, where our best colleges are engaging *freshmen* students in the hospitals, the clinics, and action arenas through which public health services are delivered. But in a city like New York, in industry, government, the arts, and technical institutions of great variety, there are exciting new possibilities for revitalizing the apprenticeship or internship concept, and building our educational programs around the relevant problems of our time. We must take steps through the new college to introduce our students in a practical way to the world of work and politics through decision-making opportunities which are relevant. We must stop regarding higher education as a pause in the life of young adults, and recast it as a vibrant and exciting part of adult life.

Finally, the new community college should recognize that although the older generation do have something they alone can convey to the younger, what the young may teach each other is at least as important. We must come to honor the capacity of the young adult to run his own life, to share in the direction of institutions specially created for him. We must honor not only his capacity to learn, but to learn by teaching others. Institutions which are for the young must honor and respect the young.

At the dawn of universal advanced education, on the threshold of open admissions, our university, in the nation's greatest city, has an extraordinary opportunity to pioneer, to create a new kind of college for the community in an urban style, in the style of those who will soon be the majority of our people, in the style of the future.

I have faith in the leadership of this university to rise to the challenge. I have faith in the future of this city. But most of all, I have faith in the young who are the students at the Staten Island Community College, and in the community which supports this college. So long as I am president in this system here, I pledge myself not only to revere the past, but also to work for the new, to strive for the young, and to pursue the truth as we see it together—whatever the risk.

I would like now to ask the faculty of Staten Island Community College, here present, to rise.

I say to this assembly and to the community which supports this college, behold these men and women! They are reason for rejoicing. Their dedication and intelligence celebrate this college.

To this faculty I say: Thanks for this occasion. You honor me, and I will do the best I can.

I would like to ask those students of this college here present to rise.

I say to this assembly and to the community which supports this college, behold these young people! They are why we are here. Celebrate them even as you respect yourselves, for they are the future you have produced. Have faith in them even as those who teach them do, for they promise to be better than you and I.

To you students, I say, I am here to serve you, to help you be yourselves, which is your ultimate aspiration—and mine.

I would like to ask Arleigh Williamson and Horace Kallen to stand.

I say to this assembly, behold these men!

Arleigh Williamson, age eighty-one, distinguished member of the Board of Higher Education, founder of this college and others, professor emeritus of New York University, leading and revered citizen of this city and this borough.

Horace Kallen, age eighty-seven, honored student and partner of William James, distinguished professor emeritus of the New School for Social Research and Columbia University, author of more than a score of great books, philosopher honored in all lands.

Behold these men. They are great teachers of your new president and even now, in the agility of their minds and the youth of their spirits, they are as young or younger than their student.

To the younger people here I say: Look at these men and wonder about the meaning of age, about being wise and about being young, about the bridge of wisdom which spans the gaps not of generations but of epochs.

Behold these men, and if you will, grow young by being wise, and grow wise through those simple and decent things which are ageless.

Finally, I would like Charles Birenbaum to stand up.

Charles is my son and he is twelve years old. He plays soccer and the cello, and he writes poems. He wrote a poem for his dad to commemorate this occasion. It reads:

> Everyman needs a heart,
> To reach into,
> To pull out the very soul
> Which blooms in his mind.

He needs a heart,
to light the fire,
The fire of life which burns
In the core of his knowledge.

He needs a mind,
To know the meaning
Of war and of hatred—
And of love.

He needs a mind,
To reach into,
To touch the core of his being—
His reason to live in a world made by man.

To this assembly and the community which supports this college, I say: Behold, Charles, at the age of twelve, thinks thoughts which never occurred to your new president when he was twelve.

To the students of this college, to whom the future belongs, I say: Behold Charles, to whom your version of the future may seem as unacceptable as mine does to you.

Let us celebrate, therefore, the meaning of ourselves on this occasion. For from Charles at twelve to Professor Williamson at eighty-one and Dr. Kallen at eighty-seven there is a direct line into the meaning of this event and the meaning of this college. We need each other, all four. Through this simple truth we may yet—black and white, young and old, teacher and taught, town and gown—do something together of which we will be proud.

BEYOND THE DILEMMA [11]

KENNETH B. CLARK [12]

Three years ago, Whitney M. Young, Jr., executive director of the National Urban League, spoke at Cambridge, Massachusetts, before a meeting of the Joint Center for Urban Studies. His thesis was that the central cities "of this increasingly urban nation are not only threatened with collapse, but are, in fact, collapsing, in large part due to the fiscal disease of the ghetto. [Consequently] what we are confronted with in the civil rights struggle is no longer a problem for the Negro alone, but for the whole society." Moreover, "if there is no genuine conviction about the rightness of integration and human relations and no will to arrive at solutions —then laws alone cannot solve the problem—and the future welfare of our cities is in serious jeopardy."

In the concise and acutely penetrating speech reprinted here, Kenneth B. Clark also dealt with the "pathology of the ghetto"; but he reflected particularly on the depth of racism in America, on the shocking human—let alone economic—costs of continued school segregation, and on the "moral confusions" and tragic consequences arising from the unresolved problem of racism in our society. At one point in this address, which was given before a joint meeting in New York City on April 29-30, 1970, of the Academy of Religion and Mental Health and the Metropolitan Research Center, Dr. Clark concluded:

> It is my considered judgment—based upon the evidence of the past fifteen years—that American society will not effectively desegregate its schools—or mount a serious attack against racism and racial polarization generally—as long as it views these problems primarily in terms of their damage to Negroes, and to Negro children. The history of racism has prepared many, if not the majority, of Americans psychologically to accept injury to—or the outright expendability of—Negro children.
>
> The argument for desegregation of our public schools must, therefore, be presented now in terms of the damage which racially segregated schools—and racism as a whole— imposes upon privileged white children.

[11] Address given before the conference of the Academy of Religion and Mental Health and the Metropolitan Applied Research Center, Inc., April 29-30, 1970, in New York City. Text furnished by Dr. Clark, with permission for this reprint.

[12] For biographical note, see Appendix.

Dr. Clark is a widely recognized and highly esteemed authority on civil rights. Since 1942 he has been a member of the psychology department at the City College of New York. He has combined his duties as a professor of psychology with active participation in community and national programs, both as a researcher and as an administrator. He founded the Northside Center for Child Development; was actively involved in the work of Harlem Youth Opportunities Unlimited, and is currently president of the Metropolitan Applied Research Center, Inc. He supplied a considerable amount of the scientific information upon which the United States Supreme Court based its decision of May 17, 1954, in *Brown v. Board of Education of Topeka,* holding that "separate educational facilities are inherently unequal."

In terms of what has happened to the country—and to me —in the interim, it seems a very long time ago that I agreed, as a young graduate student, to work with my former teacher, Ralph Bunche, and Gunnar Myrdal on the project that was to result in *An American Dilemma.*

Much of the data in that report is now superseded; many of the findings may seem naïve in terms of our new realism about the depth of American racism. But the basic truths of that study have not been superseded and there is still an American dilemma, more frightening now than it seemed even then—and still unresolved.

The pathology of the ghetto is now clear and recognized —the statistics of infant mortality, disease, rat infestation, broken plumbing, littered streets, consumer exploitation, riot-burned buildings that have not been replaced, inefficient schools, a discriminatory system of police and court procedures. The litany of pain and despair is the same in every dark ghetto and, despite the antipoverty programs, Title I funds, model cities, and so on, the ghetto is still dark and still desperate.

We must now go beyond that litany to think, and conceive, and plan alternatives. If one assumes that the ghetto cannot survive as a ghetto if our cities are to survive, and that our nation cannot survive if the cities die, we have no choice *but* to create alternatives. We must face certain hard questions: Should we seek to disband and disperse the ghetto or reinforce it? What will be the possibilities of choice for human beings who are now confined to the prison of the ghetto? Will Scarsdale, White Plains, Bethesda, Grosse Point, or Newton make room for them? Or will scattered-site ghettos be built in the suburbs near the highways, or dumps, inconvenient to transportation lines, isolated from residential property? There is considerable evidence that the suburban Negro finds himself once again isolated or evicted in behalf of urban renewal, pushed out to another less affluent town that cannot afford to exclude him.

We need to consider *all* of the costs of the ghetto—whether it is more costly to retain or to abolish the ghetto; whether it is more costly to reinforce separatism—perhaps with a cordoned force—or to choose genuine integration. It may be that there is no choice between these two stark alternatives. We may well find that the answers are surprising—that the ghetto costs more than an integrated society even simply in terms of financial burden to the city—in terms of property that cannot support an adequate tax base, unproductive land, decaying utilities, damaged and unproductive persons.

It has always been apparent that the human costs of the ghetto could not be borne. What has been less clear is the extent of the human costs of the segregated affluent suburb too often corroded by its artificial isolation. The pathology of the ghetto itself has been recorded and does not need to be recorded again. No one who knows this tragic record can accept the fallacy and glib slogan of benign neglect—to relate that concept to America's dark ghettos betrays a profound deficiency and distortion of perception. It betrays the failure of many whites to understand that the ghetto will be neglected at their own peril, that whites must cope with racial problems *for their own sake*. The solution of the ghetto is tied to their own survival. *This* is the dilemma beyond the dilemma.

The price of racism in America is high and all must pay it—the victimizers as well as the victims, for the pathology of the ghetto cannot be contained. The drugs which lulled Harlem youth into a false euphoria have spread to Westchester; urban blight is creeping toward the suburbs like a steady plague. The riots and disruptions that burned the heart of many of the nation's largest cities from 1965 to 1967, spread to smaller cities and suburbs in 1968 and 1969.

Racism has many distinguishing characteristics, but none among them is more deeply necessary to the racist psychology than self-deception. The black nationalist who tells himself that he is "together" and proud—but who fears to face whites in competition in the classroom or the job; the black "militant" leader who exploits the frustrations of his own people in cynical alliance with segregationists; the white segregationist who justifies his rejection of other human beings, citing alleged evidence of Negro inferiority; the white liberal who defends his double-standard support of black separatism on benevolent grounds; the white public official who recommends benign neglect of the poor and the despairing—all these share in a dangerous fantasy that leads to self-destruction of the spirit, and corrupts and subverts a free society. This pattern of fantasies is the core of the contemporary American dilemma.

The American dilemma, as defined by Gunnar Myrdal, was the dilemma of ideals betrayed in practice. The dilemma beyond the dilemma is also essentially a dilemma of America's whites, who have the power to turn America around but have so far been unwilling to assume the costs of justice even in behalf of their own survival.

To focus on the dilemma as it is exemplified in the area of education: On May 17 of this year it will be sixteen years since the United States Supreme Court concluded, in *Brown v. Board of Education of Topeka*

. . . That in the field of public education the doctrine of "separate but equal" has no place. Separate educational facilities are inherently unequal.

In arriving at this conclusion, the Court cited modern psychological knowledge as to the detrimental effect of racial
segregation in public schools on minority-group children.
It stated:

To separate them from others of similar age and qualifications
solely because of their race generates a feeling of inferiority as to
their status in the community that may affect their hearts and
minds in a way unlikely ever to be undone.

With these words the United States Supreme Court established the basis and rationale for subsequent discussion
of, and actions and evasions related to, the desegregation of
the public schools—namely, that segregated schools violated
the constitutional rights of Negro students—to equal protection of the laws—by damaging them, educationally and psychologically. The evidence of such detriment and damage
had received judicial sanction.

Nevertheless, during the fifteen years that followed, this
approach failed to touch the conscience of the masses of
American people—and failed to arouse the type of serious
action and social change designed to save human beings
from sustained cruelty and damage.

Instead, public officials and educational officials sought
a variety of ways of procrastination, evasion, tokenism.
Some talked of "cultural deprivation" and decided that the
schools could not assume the burden of teaching reading
until the "deprived culture" was transformed. Some, like
President Nixon, decried the effort to "demand too much
of our schools. . . . not only to educate, but also to accomplish a social transformation."

Some flirted with the speculations of the new, and re-
gressive racial geneticists who claim to have confirmed in-
nate Negro inferiority. Some gave priority to the racial
anxieties of whites and hence opposed programs of school
pairing or bussing or educational parks.

I repeat—with a sense of profound concern about the
humanity and morality of my fellow Americans—that the
knowledge that segregated schools inflicted permanent dam-

age upon Negro children was not enough to compel the American people to plan and implement a massive and effective program for the desegregation of our public schools.

For the masses of white Americans, it appears that Negro children are clearly expendable.

As the desegregation struggle moved from the South to the North it resulted in white backlash and in black separatism—two sides of the same coin—and it resulted in a tragic series of urban ghetto disruptions.

Recent urban riots and racial polarization in America can be viewed as symptoms of the increased frustrations resulting from unfulfilled promises inherent in the *Brown* decision. These disturbances and more overt forms of racism are a more intense and focused sign of the detrimental consequences of the continuation of racially stigmatized segregated schools in a segregated society.

But it is my considered judgment—based upon the evidence of the past fifteen years—that American society will not effectively desegregate its schools—or mount a serious attack against racism and racial polarization generally—as long as it views these problems primarily in terms of their damage to Negroes, and to Negro children. The history of racism has prepared many, if not the majority, of Americans psychologically to accept injury to—or the outright expendability of Negro children.

The argument for desegregation of our public schools must, therefore, be presented now in terms of the damage which racially segregated schools—and racism as a whole—imposes upon privileged white children.

There is strong evidence to suggest that racial segregation —the institutionalization of racism—is flagrantly and insidiously detrimental to white children, as well as to black. And I do not believe that the masses of American whites wish to inflict damage upon their own children.

Ironically, the United States Supreme Court, in the *Brown* case, had before it evidence suggesting that segregation did damage white children. In the social science brief appended to the legal brief it was stated in discussing the detrimental effects of racism on white children:

. . . The culture permits and, at times, encourages them to direct their feelings of hostility and aggression against whole groups of people, the members of which are perceived as weaker than themselves. They often develop patterns of guilt feelings, rationalizations, and other mechanisms which they must use in an attempt to protect themselves from recognizing the essential injustice of their unrealistic fears and hatreds of minority groups.

The report indicates further that confusion, conflict, moral cynicism, and disrespect for authority may arise in majority-group children as a consequence of being taught the moral, religious and democratic principles of the brotherhood of man and the importance of justice and fair play by the same persons and institutions who, in their support of racial segregation and related practices, seem to be acting in a prejudiced and discriminatory manner. These ideas were first examined in 1950 and written in 1952. They may be viewed as prophetic of the current youth rebellion.

Let us examine some of the moral confusions posed for individuals who are required to cope with the dilemma of racism in a verbally democratic society:

1. The attempt to escape personal guilt, through the use of a variety of forms of self-protection and rationalizations —including reinforcing racism and blaming the victims of racism for their predicament

2. Moral cynicism and rejection of all values—the development of a dog-eat-dog philosophy of life

3. The effort to avoid a sense of moral and ethical emptiness which a racist—racially segregated—society imposes upon all sensitive human beings

4. Rejection of authority

5. The moral and ethical conflict created when one is compelled to serve as an accessory to racial segregation and cruelty imposed upon others; when one is forced to be an involuntary beneficiary of such cruelty

These are merely some of the symptoms of cruelty—the moral

schizophrenia inflicted upon sensitive individuals as they struggle to avoid the personal disruptions inherent in this socially imposed ethical conflict.

It is a realistic and accepted tragedy that the majority of American youth accommodate to the normative hypocrisy, accept the rationalizations, the explanations, the excuses for the racism of the larger society. These "adjusted" young people function in terms of the philosophy of dog-eat-dog and every man for himself. They may experience an intensification of feelings of hostility and contempt toward minorities—and all others who are perceived as weak—and often act out these feelings in cruel, insensitive and at times immoral behavior.

On the other hand, a growing but critical minority of white American youth appear to be suffering from intense personal guilt feelings, and, therefore, seem compelled to rebel against parents, established leaders, institutions. Some of these young people sometimes adopt a cynical rejection of all moral values, all ethics as having no value other than the verbal and the exploitative. For these anguished young people, moral values and even rationality are seen as inevitably contaminated—as tools of immorality—for the hypocritical establishment and therefore must be rejected. This poses a most critical danger for a stable democratic society.

The contemporary racial dilemma, now mocking or challenging America, comes in the forms of the illusive malaise of the privileged—the affluent—white youth:

—The hippie movement with its random, chaotic, search for ethical clarity and consistency;

—The drug cult of the middle-class youth who seek escape from intolerable ethical emptiness;

—The hostility and aggression expressed toward parents and other authorities who inflicted, or permitted this conflict to be inflicted, upon them;

—The new-left-quasi-anarchistic movement among youth; with its hostile, often self-destructive expressions that seek to destroy that which is perceived as a social process systematically destroying the ethical substance and potential within them;

—The campus rebellions which, like urban ghetto riots, may be seen as the counterattack by a critical minority of American youth against a system of intolerable moral hypocrisy and ethical inconsistency.

For these young people, the system is not made tolerable by their affluence—by parental indulgence, by educational permissiveness—even by owning their own car; nor is it made tolerable by the deadening law and order offered by many homogeneous suburban communities in lieu of ethical substance and demonstrated democracy.

Segregated schools, and the tyranny and barbarity of American ghettos, are the institutionalized inescapable immorality of American racism. And, as such, segregated schools are stultifying and destroying the ethical and personal effectiveness of American white children more insidiously than they are destroying the personal and human effectiveness of America's black children—who, at least, understand what is done to them and many, therefore, can continue the struggle against this type of dehumanization.

If colleges and universities understood this, they would reorganize, modifying their governance structure if necessary in order to intervene directly to improve dramatically and rapidly the quality and efficiency of education for rejected black children. They would find a way to move into deprived public schools in a supervisory, accountability and evaluative role. They would demand that elementary and secondary public schools cease to be educational disaster areas.

They would, in addition, develop to help white students —the white student from the less privileged background and more privileged whites from affluent families—to help them broaden their perspective of man away from the constricted racist perspective of their parents and peers.

The anxieties and insecurities of blue-collar and white-collar whites are important factors in the random hostilities and cruelties of racism. Colleges and universities must assume the specific task of education to liberate white youth from this important form of moral and ethical disadvantage.

If public officials understood the special needs of ethically disadvantaged white youth, they would be less prone, I believe, to procrastinate, to equivocate and mouth the hypocrisy against "bussing" or transporting children for integrated education.

If they understood this, they would be less prone to talk the rhetoric of black capitalism or white supremacy—subtle or flagrant—support segregated black studies, pay out meaningless reparations at the same time that they fail to change American society; to talk compensatory education and cultural deprivation and all other language of narrow racial identity without planning for serious change.

If they understood this, they would build an agenda for a future—their own future, a future for all Americans.

America has the resources to move beyond the stagnant dilemma of the present. An America who could mobilize resources to land men on the moon, could mobilize its financial, material, intellectual and human resources to wage a serious war against slums and poverty and eliminate all institutionalized forms of racism within the decade of the 1970s.

There could be no more fitting goal in the celebration of America's bicentennial than to make the egalitarian promises of Jefferson real for all Americans—black as well as white —by 1976. The specific targets essential for attaining this goal are:

—effective nonracial schools, with teachers who teach and children who learn

—housing, worthy of human beings, in our urban and rural areas

—jobs—consistent with human dignity

—an elimination of the need and concept and stigma of welfare

—health services in terms of need rather than ability to pay.

Our society can and must provide for all of its citizens such minimal symbols of the respect of human beings for human beings as clean streets, adequate public transportation, useful and stimulating parks and cultural and recreational facilities; and all of those things which are essential to eliciting those esthetic and creative and ethical potentials of man.

The costs will be high but the alternative costs of a divided, and dying and dehumanizing society will be far greater. This is the dilemma beyond the dilemma.

INDIAN AFFAIRS—WHAT HAS BEEN DONE AND WHAT NEEDS TO BE DONE [13]

WENDELL CHINO [14]

A long overdue recognition of the American Indians' contribution to the national culture seems in sight. The Indians are speaking more vigorously in their own behalf; non-Indians are joining more actively in the dialogue. Perhaps for the first time, the Indians are getting a sympathetic press, a wide public notice of their immense talents and resources, and a more general appreciation of their role in the shaping of our national experience. Distorted views of the Indian and his values and ways of life are, it is hoped, being changed. This should result in a more faithful revelation of the inner nature and power of this remarkable group of people. In a modest way, the Indian Studies Programs at certain colleges are helping to correct the old, false impressions. And the achievements of such accomplished writers as N. Scott Momaday, Pulitzer Prize winner for fiction in 1969, enhance the public appreciation of the universal values in the lore and fact and custom of the Indian culture.

Associated with this cultural awakening is the growing demand by Indians for a fuller share of the nation's bounties and in the management of their own lives. About three quarters of a million Indians and Eskimos live in the United States. Of that number, some 450,000 live on reservations distributed throughout the country in twenty-six states; the rest are concentrated largely in the urban centers. The total land holdings of the Indians on reservations is down to about 56,000,000 acres. The economic, health, and education problems of the Indian population are grave. And they explain in part the signs of militancy and assertions of Indian power which the younger Indian leadership especially is currently voicing. In response to these conditions, President Nixon issued a detailed statement in July 1970, beginning with these reflections:

> The first Americans—the Indians—are the most deprived and most isolated minority in our nation. On virtually every scale of measurement—employment, income,

[13] Address delivered at the annual convention of the National Congress of American Indians on October 6, 1969, at Albuquerque, New Mexico. Text furnished by the Rev. Mr. Chino, with permission for this reprint.

[14] For biographical note, see Appendix.

education, health—the condition of the Indian people ranks at the bottom.

This condition is the heritage of centuries of injustice. From the time of their first contact with European settlers, the American Indians have been oppressed and brutalized, deprived of their ancestral lands and denied the opportunity to control their own destiny. Even the Federal programs which are intended to meet their needs have frequently proved to be ineffective and demeaning. But the story of the Indian in America is something more than the record of the white man's frequent aggression, broken agreements, intermittent remorse and prolonged failure. It is a record also of endurance, of survival, of adaptation and creativity in the face of overwhelming obstacles. It is a record of enormous contributions to this country—to its art and culture, to its strength and spirit, to its sense of history and its sense of purpose.

In the 1963-1964 edition of REPRESENTATIVE AMERICAN SPEECHES appeared a speech by Raymond Nakai, chairman of the Navajo Tribal Council. Reprinted here is an address by another noted leader, Wendell Chino, the president of the Mescalero Apache Tribe. Mr. Chino was president of the National Congress of American Indians and chairman of the New Mexico Commission on Indian Affairs. This keynote address was delivered at the twenty-fifth annual convention of the National Congress of American Indians on October 6, 1969, at Albuquerque, New Mexico.

In the face of the agony of the Vietnam war, revolution for relevance, and revolution of racial hatred, our country has made tremendous progress in the fields of science and technology. We can send a man to the moon, we can go to the depths of the sea and probe its darkness. We have learned to harness the energy of the sun and use its energy, and we can build giant computers. So—we stop and take stock of our achievements—a technology that very few nations of the world can match. In spite of progress and advancements—we are failing in, and have neglected our primary duty to our people, and especially among our people—the American Indian.

I share the very deep common concern we all feel and have felt for these troubled and terrible conditions in our country and the world. Today, we, the American Indian people are faced with many problems—political, economic, financial, racial, and many more. As an individual, I am a concerned citizen of this country—the country, which, in spite of its failings, that I love so very much. Indeed, I want to do everything that I can to promote its welfare and to see that it does not neglect its people.

Therefore, I want to address myself to: Indian Affairs—what has been done and what is remaining to be done.

From that first historic encounter between the American Indians and the "white men," our Indian lands have been diminished, leaving only certain allotted lands and estab-lished reservations as the remaining land base for the American Indians.

The Congress of the United States assumed responsibility for the Indian people. That responsibility included their education, health, and their general welfare. After almost two hundred years, we are even more cognizant of this responsi-bility and the commitment to our people and the great job which still needs to be done.

In addition to the concern and the responsibility of the Federal Government, certain Indian-interest groups and non-Indian individuals have made numerous reports on the ad-ministration of Indian affairs. We have been studied to death by reports and task forces representing the expenditure of vast sums of money. With this expenditure to improve our conditions you would think that we ought to be better off than we are today with all the reports and recommendations made in our behalf, suggesting ways and means of improv-ing our conditions and welfare.

The changes in the Administration of this country have made the Indian people and their problems a political foot-ball resulting in vacillating policies. Some Administrations advocated keeping the status quo by leaving Indian matters and policies like they have been for a good many years. Some Administrations have initiated action requiring premature withdrawals of Federal services to the Indian people in several states—perhaps in more of the states, if the National Congress of American Indians and their friends had not intervened in certain cases in behalf of the Indian people. A review of the present condition of certain "terminated tribes" does not speak well of the Federal Government and its termination policy.

In view of these seemingly adverse and weak efforts by all parties concerned, we need now to look ahead and ask ourselves, What needs to be done in Indian affairs?

Since all of the studies and reviews reflect the weakness of the Bureau of Indian Affairs and the reticence of the Congress to deeply concern itself with the Indian people and their problems, then, in line with our theme, we must become involved! There is no other recourse but to stress the need for a strong, positive leadership among our Indian Tribes, pueblos and groups. If you see a need or a job that is waiting to be accomplished—put your hands to the plow, then having put your hands to the plow, request assistance if you need it. The need of this hour among Indian people is for strong, positive leadership that must come to grips with local problems—leadership that must be heard on state and national levels. It is not enough to speak only of our ills and the shortcomings of the Bureau of Indian Affairs—let us provide the leadership to provide the motivation and the stimulation to attack those areas needing our time, energy and effort.

Whether we are reservation or urban Indians—radicals or conservatives, we are Indians—let us not knock one another or seek personal aggrandizement. Let us, with common interest and energy make united efforts to attack those problems affecting our people. Unite we must—lest we divide and lose our strength.

Another thing that needs special attention is to secure from the Congress, an annual appropriation that is realistic, and large enough to attack and combat our problems. At the present rate of appropriation for Indian programs, it will take centuries to accomplish the task mutually facing all of us.

Turning our attention to the new national Administration, I have some remarks to address to it:

The "New Federalism" advocated by the new Administration has no appeal or interest for me as presently enunciated and I'll tell you why. The concept of the New Federalism that I hear is that all grants-in-aid and all Federal funding of projects and programs are going to be channeled through the states. By channeling funds through the states, the Federal Government will be abrogating its responsibility, a primary and a constitutional responsibility, to the several states for administration. I do believe that this form of the New Federalism will not work to the benefit of the American Indians, in fact, it will work against them. It will put all of us out in the cold!

New Federalism could work for the Indian people if it is handled in the right way. For New Federalism to work among the Indian tribes, those tribes must be dealt with on the same basis as the several states. Federal assistance must be granted to the Indian tribes in the same way that it is granted to the states—directly! For Federal Indian help to be channeled through the states will result in only tokenism. We need only to look at the administration of funds appropriated under the Omnibus Crime Law. Have any of our tribes really gained or received *any* benefits from this law, a law which grants funds to the several states for administration? At Mescalero, we have not received one iota of service or benefit from the Federal grant to the state of New Mexico.

Instead of New Federalism and tokenism for Indian people, there must come and there must be direct funding to tribes for Indian programs. The Indian desks now existing in the various departments of the Government must remain and continue; in fact, we need more of them.

The Congress of the United States must, without question, proceed immediately to enact Senate Concurrent Resolution 34, a resolution enunciating a new national Indian policy which is being spearheaded by Senator McGovern and his other senatorial colleagues. This proposed national Indian policy statement by the Congress concerning the First American must be enunciated very clearly and positively. It is a new policy that will lay to rest all the hidden and known fears manifest to us because we just do not know where we stand in our unique relationship with the Federal Government. I do not believe that this decade should come to a close without a marked improvement for our Indian people!

The Congress, through this resolution, and its disavowal of the Termination policy will restore the confidence of the Indian people in the Federal Government, making it possible for the Indian tribes and the Federal Government to go forward together to brighter future for our people and all people of this great country. The Indian must have the right of self-determination on the selection of his way of life! . . .

Let us not be lulled into accepting programs from the states!

Most of our Indian people do not now have, nor have we ever had political or legal relations with state governments. We do not now receive state assistance in any form except for those Federal funds given to the states specifically for Indians. Our experience with the states' administration of Federal funds in behalf of Indians has not been good. Only recently have we been allowed the vote in many states and today few of our Indian people do vote in state elections and have no power base in the state political machines.

The first Congress of the United States reserved unto itself, the power to deal and negotiate with Indian tribes, showing a wisdom thereby which was not fully appreciated until recent times. The Indian tribes were then, and are now legally considered as pseudosovereign nations—exercising the powers of residual sovereignty. As early as 1775, Article IX of the Articles of Confederation asserted: "The United States in Congress assembled shall also have the sole and exclusive right and power of . . . regulating the trade and managing all affairs with the Indians . . . ." This Article was approved in Congress in 1777. In 1887, the Constitution clearly established the Federal relationship to Indian tribes in the "commerce clause," which reads in part . . . "to regulate commerce with foreign nations, and among the several states, *and with the Indian tribes*."

Subsequently, Congress passed a series of Federal laws "to regulate trade and intercourse with the Indian tribes, and to preserve peace on the frontier," such laws were commonly known as the Indian Trade and Intercourse Acts which served to further clarify the *absolute* relationship between the Federal Government and the Indian tribes, *and excluded the interference of any state*. The Federal Government was anxious then to promote Indian friendship and prosperity because it needed the might of the Indian warriors allied with the Government in the fight against European colonialism. The few thousand American whites could not stand against several million Indians at their backs and several million Europeans at their shores.

Recently, a brief article appeared, stating, and I quote— "Approximately $525 million has been allotted by the Government for Indian Affairs for fiscal 1970. If that money were given directly to the heads of Indian households, they would be receiving an annual income of almost $6,000. (There are about 100,000 Indian heads of households and not more than a half million Indians in the United States.) At present, their average annual income is under $2,000." End of quotation. That is a nice thought, but the writer failed to realize that the major portion or share of the $525 million will go to maintain, sustain and perpetuate an empire of the Federal Government—the empire of the Bureau of Indian Affairs. Parenthetically, we have offered, through our NCAI position paper, ideas that we believe could provide solutions to the problem of getting more funds into the hands of the tribes, and the elimination of a bureaucracy.

This great country which we call the United States of America would not have been created without Indian participation and Indian help. During the Revolutionary War, the Federal Army invited the assistance, the cooperation and the participation of the Six Nation Confederacy, the Delawares, Wyandots, Chippewas, the Ottawas and the Shawnees to protect the northern and western fronts, and the Chero-kees, Choctaws, Creeks and Chickasaws to protect the south-ern front against the invasion of the British army.

The Indians did such an outstanding job that it resulted in total victory for the United Colonies. Thus, was the foun-dation of this country saved by the Indians. Had the Federal Army been defeated, then, there would never have been a United States of America. The early colonists looked to the Iroquois Confederacy for the formation and framing of the United States Constitution—one of the greatest and mightiest documents this world has ever known. Again, it was Indian help and Indian influence through the Iroquois Confederacy that provided the mold for the Constitution of the United States of America.

In the war with Japan, the Japanese could not decode the Navajo language, this was one code that they could not break. What a vital role the Indian language played in the Second World War—not to mention the large percentage of Indians who served in that war.

This is the kind of Indian involvement that we need. We will not accept anything less!

Now, how sad, how ironic, that our people—the Amer-ican Indians, who have certainly played a viable and vital role in the shaping of this great country—can be given only lip service by the leaders of our country, and in many cases, by the leaders of our states.

We are sick, tired, and disappointed with tokenism, political platitudes and promises that were never intended to be kept! It is going to take more than lip service from our Government, more than political tokenism from the leaders of our country to improve and accomplish the needed pro-grams existing among our people today.

What about the pledges given to the American Indians at last year's convention in Omaha, Nebraska? How many, can we truthfully say have been kept or fulfilled to the satisfac-tion of our Indian people? We are sad that all of our pleading, prodding, and requests have been shrugged off and fallen on deaf ears to be ignored.

Our pleas on behalf of our people aren't shallow or slight, they affect the basic well-being of our people. Our request for better and greater service is not welfare or tokenism! We are asking that the historic commitment of 1775 to the Indian people be fulfilled in this century.

Finally—I say to our Indian leaders and our Indian people, let *your* people see *you* take an active part in Indian affairs, and be involved in salvaging the ideals of our people, the traditions of our people. Fight the non-Indian values that would destroy our culture, and *oppose* the platitudes of our time and of the dominant society. Our mutual concern and protection will preserve and sustain our Indian heritage and culture for generations to come.

Thank you.

A FRESH LOOK AT AN OLD SPEECH

LINCOLN'S RHETORICAL TRIUMPH
AT COOPER UNION [1]

EVERETT LEE HUNT [2]

On February 27, 1960, the Cooper Union in New York City celebrated the centennial of Lincoln's appearance in its Great Hall. It was a gala event. Cooper Union issued a special edition of Lincoln's address, with an introduction by Leroy H. Buckingham; Dr. Edwin S. Burdell, then president of Cooper Union, spoke briefly on the theme of "February 27, 1860"; the Caldwell Singers presented choral music of Lincoln's time; a brass band played pieces from the pre-Civil War period; Broadway actor Ford Rainey read passages from Lincoln's speech; and the late Senator Everett M. Dirksen gave the principal address on "the man from Illinois." Mr. Dirksen closed his oration with these words:

> The Man from Illinois still speaks to his countrymen. So long as Providence endows his countrymen with the capacity to remember, he shall continue to speak to them, even as he spoke to them here one hundred years ago this night. The Man from Illinois—his name was Abraham Lincoln.

The Cooper Union opened in July 1859. Founded by Peter Cooper, industrialist and civic leader, it soon established itself—and remains so today—as one of the most exciting forums for ideas in America, and as a true pioneer in the adult education movement. The Great Hall has been host to many of America's greatest speakers, including Wendell Phillips, Frederick Douglass, Carl Schurz, Henry Ward Beecher, Theodore Roosevelt. Cooper Union is indeed a superb institution in which responsible controversy and debate have flourished for 110 years.

Little wonder, then, that teachers of speech have an uncommon interest in the Cooper Union platform. At the 1969 convention of the Speech Communication Association, a special program, sponsored by the Rhetoric and Public Address Interest Group,

---

[1] Speech delivered at Cooper Union, New York City, on December 29, 1969, before a meeting sponsored by the Rhetoric and Public Address Interest Group of the Speech Communication Association. Text furnished by Mr. Hunt, with permission for this reprint.

[2] For biographical note, see Appendix.

was held on December 29 at the Union to memorialize the contribution of the institution to American oratory. One of the speakers on the program was Everett Lee Hunt, dean emeritus of Swarthmore College. Mr. Hunt appraised the Lincoln address and concluded that it is a fine example "of the Aristotelian faculty of discovering all the available means of persuasion in a given case."

The editor derives a special pleasure from including Mr. Hunt's speech in this collection. Everett Hunt is one of the most distinguished members of the speech education profession. His keen insights and orderly analyses of the rhetorical art have greatly contributed to the establishment of speech as an intellectually respectable, humane discipline in the enterprise of learning. For over fifty years his name has been honored by all who respect the tradition of our subject and who see in it a proper and useful instrument for the disposition of human affairs in a democratic society.

Lincoln's Address here at Cooper Union on February 27, 1860, was described as a "triumph" by many notables who heard it; by journalists who reported it and distributed a million copies; by contemporary politicians who invited him to repeat his triumph in New England cities; and even by the overmodest Lincoln himself, who said that this speech, together with the photograph taken at the time and distributed with the speech, had made him President.

These contemporary judgments have been confirmed by historians who have related his speech to subsequent events, who agree that it made the little known "prairie politician" a national figure, that it unified the Republican party by reinforcing its arguments against slavery, that the doctrine of constitutional power to restrict slavery was really old and traditional, and that this doctrine justified resistance to both the Dred Scott Decision and to the Douglas doctrine of "popular sovereignty." The historical judgment, then, is that the Cooper Union Address was a political triumph in that it gave power to the convictions that restricted slavery and saved the Union.

From the contemporary and the historical let us pass on briefly to the literary judgment, which in spite of its admission that literary tastes change, asserts that the literary judg-

ment is concerned chiefly with the permanent. Literary critics have not pronounced the Cooper Union Address a triumph; they do not quote its phrases; but they do praise it by
saying that it has no "rhetorical embellishments." They assert
that for them Lincoln endures chiefly as an artist, that the
remembered phrases of his Farewell to the People of Springfield, the Inaugurals, and the Gettysburg Address, will survive all controversial issues and make Lincoln a Man of the
Ages. But these literary critics also admit that the literary
interest taken in the best and last of his works must be associated with the life of the man; for Lincoln, many assert, did
not try deliberately to be an artist, but wrote only to communicate his thoughts and emotions. These have fascinated
biographers, historians, literary critics, and, more recently,
psychoanalysts, who attempt to account for his "philosophy
of common sense."

Can it add anything to the historical, political and artis-
tic judgments of the Cooper Union Address if we add the
term *rhetorical* to the accounts of his triumph? Must we
always accept the derogatory meaning attached to the word
rhetoric in its greatly increasing contemporary usage? Should
we be implying that Lincoln was merely more skillful than
his competitors in taking the stands that would win the most
votes? Or have we reason to believe that his firm moral convictions rose above political expediency and that rhetoric and
ethics were combined in his conviction that moral issues
could be persuasive to public sentiment, and that if they were
not he would be willing to accept defeat?

Let us first consider the logic and rhetoric of his persuasive appeal to his immediate audience, and also weigh
the effect upon the country at large. Lincoln certainly never
knew of Aristotle's definition of rhetoric as the faculty of
discovering all the available means of persuasion in a given
case, but he had been exercising this faculty all his adult
life, with skillful adaptations to audiences of differing interests, degrees of intelligence and cultural background. For
example, he did not know in advance the exact nature of the

Cooper Union audience, as he had accepted the invitation
to speak at Henry Ward Beecher's Plymouth Church, but
he naturally expected they would be urban intellectuals in
sympathy with Henry Ward Beecher. The Young Republicans who changed the meeting to the Cooper Union did
bring together a large and distinguished audience of New
York Republicans who have been characterized in such detail
by so many historians that we need not name and describe
them again here.

An issue which united speaker and audience was the
doctrine of popular sovereignty as presented by Stephen
Douglas in his speeches over the country, and in the Lincoln-
Douglas debates, and shortly after (September 1859) in
a long and widely read article in *Harper's Magazine*. This
was the first attempt of a statesman to present a considered
historical argument in a popular magazine. Many of the New
York audience had read the article with bewildered disapproval. When Lincoln read it he was moved to spend many
weeks of solitary historical research in the Springfield State
Library establishing the authenticity of his belief that the
Fathers of the Constitution believed they had the right to
restrict slavery from the territories. His long, legal, historical,
and almost tedious presentation reflected his own research,
but was also the most persuasive approach to this particular
audience. It created a faith in him as a sound thinker in support of his and their moral convictions.

The student of Lincoln's rhetoric will note with interest
that the enthusiastic reception in New York led to invitations
to speak in eight New England cities, where he spoke with
more wit and spontaneity in presenting the same convictions.
In addition to the repetition of the speech before other audiences the speech was widely distributed by the press, and read
over the country.

One thing that contributed to the wide reading of Lincoln's speech was its being printed together with a speech by
his chief rival for the Republican nomination, William H.
Seward, delivered in the Senate two days after Lincoln's

Cooper Union Address. Two years earlier Seward's famous "Irrepressible Conflict" speech had supported and called attention to Lincoln's "House Divided" speech. But in his Senate speech, Seward, evidently alarmed by threats of secession, softened his position by deleting all moral criticism of slavery. This allowed his critics to charge that he was merely a politician, seeking the nomination, and not a man of sincere convictions. The contrast between the two speakers, in the tension of national opinion, made Lincoln's firm stand more persuasive.

A similar persuasive factor in the speech relates to Douglas, chief Democratic contender for the presidency. Douglas had won the Illinois senatorial election largely on the appeal of his position on popular sovereignty. Lincoln had known that this doctrine would probably give Douglas the victory in Illinois, but he had said that he was looking farther ahead than the senatorial election. He foresaw that the popular sovereignty doctrine, which upset the Dred Scott Decision, upholding the right of a slave owner to take his property anywhere, would lose Douglas the support of the South—which it did, and it lost him as well the support of Buchanan and the northern Democrats who were trying to keep the Democrats a viable national party of all interests, North and South. Although there were bound to be many unpredictable complications in those nominating conventions, both Democratic and Republican, it was still true that a man with little financial support, who wrote his own speech, and ignored revisions, even those suggested by the owners of the Chicago *Tribune,* could take a strong ground with a conciliatory yet firm tone, and produce the belief that he was the one Republican who could be elected.

We should not omit a consideration of that part of the Cooper Union Address which Lincoln said was addressed to the people of the South. He knew that very few Southerners were present, but New Yorkers whose business was with southern cotton were there, and he repeated in summary form what he had said earlier in Cincinnati, on the very border of the South. It would not have been persuasive to Southerners, as it had not been previously, but his appeal (really to the North) to respect the South, to understand it, to yield everything possible without yielding in the belief that slavery was wrong, and that the Federal Government had the power to restrict it in the territories, was an appeal rising to religious heights in asking his audience not to reverse the divine rule.

Lest I have minimized the persuasive *eloquence* of the speech, let me quote some concluding lines, which, I think, deserve to be remembered with some of the more frequently quoted passages from later speeches:

> If slavery is right, all words, acts, laws and constitutions against it are themselves wrong; if it is wrong they cannot justly insist upon its extensions—its enlargement. All they ask, we could readily grant, if we thought slavery right; all we ask they could as readily grant if they thought it wrong. . . . Neither let us be slandered from our duty by false accusations against us, nor frightened from it by menaces to the Government nor of dungeons to ourselves. Let us have faith that right makes might, and in that faith let us to the end, dare to do our duty as we understand it.

Lincoln regarded this speech as the culminating statement of his pre-election position. He refused to speak during the presidential campaign. He felt he had said it, that further speeches would produce further controversies among extremists, and could add nothing to his clearly reasoned position. He had offered a program based on a concept of national power, a rejection of compromise, a refusal to accept the Dred Scott Decision and the Kansas-Nebraska Bill, and a clear program of national action to restrict slavery and unify the nation under constitutional power. Lincoln won a unanimous vote for the nomination by the Republican electors on the third ballot, as it became apparent that Seward could not be elected.

Since the Cooper Union Address was a deliberate rather than a eulogistic speech, some rhetorical critics would say that we should not look beyond the decision which followed in the election. But in assessing it today we are influenced by its consistency with the events in Lincoln's career which it produced. As we read the history of Lincoln's Administration we cannot but be impressed by the evidence that this speech reflected his personal convictions and attitudes. In the selection of his cabinet he included men of opposite positions and judged between them. In such decisions as what to do about Fort Sumter he was a model of firmness in the midst of conflicting advice. In the chaos of military disorganization he never lost his faith that right makes might. In the issues of Compensated Emancipation and especially of the Emancipation Proclamation he resisted the furor of the abolitionists who took too little thought for the future of the Negro, or of the South. Lincoln was deeply concerned for both and considered gravely how to remunerate the South for its losses, and how to increase the rights and opportunities of the Negroes. It was a concern which grew steadily upon him. Part of the national tragedy of his death is that he could not carry out these plans, so full of deliberate thought for the future of his country. His final Emancipation Proclamation was not, he knew, a solution to the Negro problem, but a military expedient for winning the war. He expected to follow it with measures which embittered congressmen probably would never have supported.

Thus later events in Lincoln's career make the Cooper Union Address prophetic of his fitness for the presidency, and suggest that his appeal for a belief that right makes might was not mere rhetoric in its contemporary sense but was a program of action based on a lofty ethic.

This Cooper Union Address was persuasive in that it was the mature expression of the characteristic beliefs and reflections of a man of sound judgment, informed by historical research, and concerned with a choice between civic goods. It argued for a middle ground which was the best possible middle ground between extremists. It appealed to the intelligence and moral convictions of his listeners. It made an American tradition out of the startling contrast between his Western frontier appearance and speech on one hand,

and his good manners, with the wisdom and common sense of his conclusions, on the other. Where can we find a better example of the Aristotelian faculty of discovering all the available means of persuasion in a given case? The Cooper Union Address was a rhetorical triumph in that it was perhaps an unprecedented combination of political skill with a nobility of purpose and lofty qualities of ethical persuasion which are a permanent need of democratic society.

APPENDIX

BIOGRAPHICAL NOTES

AGNEW, SPIRO THEODORE (1918-   ). Born, Towson, Maryland; studied chemistry three years, Johns Hopkins University; LL.B., University of Baltimore, 1947; honorary degrees in law, University of Maryland, Morgan State College, Ohio State University, and other institutions; private law practice, civic affairs, and local Republican politics in Baltimore; county executive, Baltimore County, 1962-66; teacher of night classes in law, University of Baltimore, 1959-66; elected governor of Maryland, 1966; member, executive committee, National Governors' Conference; member, Advisory Commission on Intergovernmental Relations, 1968; company commander with Tenth Armored Division, World War II; Vice President of the United States, 1969-   . (See also *Current Biography: December 1968.*)

BIRENBAUM, WILLIAM M. (1923-   ). Born, Macomb, Illinois; student, Iowa State Teachers College, 1943; LL.D., University of Chicago, 1949; director, student affairs, University of Chicago, 1949-54; member, faculty of social sciences, 1950-54; dean of students, University College, 1955-57; director of research and executive, Conference Board, Associated Research Councils, Ford Foundation project for study of post-doctoral international exchanges, 1954-55; assistant vice president, Wayne State University, 1957-61; dean, New School for Social Research, 1961-64; vice president, provost, Brooklyn Center, Long Island University, 1964-67; president, Education Affiliate, Bedford-Stuyvesant Development and Services Corporation, Brooklyn, 1967-68; president, Staten Island Community College, 1968-   ; president, Association of Community Councils, Metropolitan Chicago, 1955-57; chairman, Michigan Cultural Commission, 1960-61; founder, original director, Detroit Adventure, association of cultural institutions, 1958-61; member, Board of Education, districts 21-22, New York City, 1962-64; board of directors, Brooklyn chapter, American Civil Liberties Union, 1967-70; chairman, education committee, Metropolitan Council, American Jewish Congress, 1967-68; chairman, academic freedom committee, 1967- ; board of trustees, Friends World College, 1970- ; Little Red School House on Bleecker Street, New York City, 1963- ; board adviser, Brooklyn Academy of Music, 1965- ; board of trustees, Brooklyn Institute of Arts and Sciences, 1969- ; member, Chicago Bar Association; Delta Sigma; author, *Overlive: Power, Poverty and the University*, 1968.

BRONOWSKI, J(ACOB) (1908-). Born in Poland; M.A., Jesus College, Cambridge, 1930; Ph.D., 1933; lecturer, University College, Hull, England, 1934-42; senior scientist, Ministry of Home Security, 1942-45; assistant director, Ministry of Works, 1946-50; director, Coal Research Establishment, National Coal Board, 1950-59; director, general process development, 1959-63; in United States, 1964- ; senior fellow and trustee, Salk Institute for Biological Studies, San Diego, California; lecturer on man and nature, American Museum of Natural History, 1965; Eastman Memorial Professor, University of Rochester, 1965; Condon lecturer, Oregon State University, 1967; Silliman lecturer, Yale University, 1967; fellow, World Academy of Art and Science; American Academy of Arts and Sciences; author, *The Poet's Defence*, 1939; *William Blake: A Man Without a Mask*, 1944; *The Common Sense of Science*, 1951; *Science and Human Values*, 1956; *Insight*, 1964; *The Abacus and the Rose: A New Dialogue on Two World Systems*, 1965; *The Identity of Man*, 1965; *Nature and Knowledge*, 1969; and others. (See also *Current Biography: September 1958*.)

CHINO, REVEREND WENDELL (1923-). Born, Mescalero Indian Reservation, New Mexico; elementary education at the reservation school; high school education at Government boarding school, Santa Fe; attended Central College, Pella, Iowa, and Cook Christian Training School, Phoenix, Arizona; graduate, Western Theological Seminary, Holland, Michigan; ordained as first Apache minister by New York Classis at Reformed Church, Mescalero, New Mexico, 1951; served two terms as president of the National Congress of American Indians; chairman, New Mexico Commission on Indian Affairs, 1965-69; chairman, National Advisory Committee on Indian Education, working closely with Bureau of Indian Affairs; member, New Mexico Commission on Human Rights; chairman of board of directors, Sierra Blanca Ski Enterprise; president, Mescalero Apache Tribe.

CHURCH, FRANK (1924-   ). Born, Boise, Idaho; on debating team, Boise high school; A.B., Stanford University, 1947; LL.B., 1950; admitted to Idaho bar, 1950; practiced law in Boise, 1950-56; chairman, Crusade for Freedom, 1954, 1955; keynote speaker, state Democratic convention, 1952; United States Senate (Democrat, Idaho), 1956-   ; keynote speaker, Democratic National Convention, 1960; first lieutenant, World War II; one of ten outstanding young men, United States Junior Chamber of Commerce, 1957; recipient, American Legion Oratorical Contest Award, 1941 ("The American Way of Life"); Joffre Debate Medal, Stanford University, 1947; Phi Beta Kappa; member United States Senate Committee on Foreign Relations; Committee on Interior and Insular Affairs. (See also *Current Biography: March 1958*.)

CLARK, KENNETH B. (1914-   ). Born, Panama Canal Zone; A.B., Howard University, 1935; M.S., 1936; Ph.D., Columbia University, 1940; department of psychology, City College of New York, 1942-   ; professor, 1960-   ; visiting professor, summer, Columbia University; University of California, Berkeley; associated with National Association for the Advancement of Colored People, 1950-   ; consultant, personnel division, United States Department of State; member, committee on foreign affairs personnel, 1961-62; member, Commission on Integration, Board of Education, New York City, 1954-58; member, New York State Youth Commission; National Scholarship Service and Fund for Negro Students; director, New Lincoln School; founder, Northside Center for Child Development; Harlem Youth Opportunities Unlimited; president, Metropolitan Applied Research Center, Inc.; member, Board of Regents, New York State; member, board of trustees, Howard University; former member, board of trustees, Antioch College; recipient, Spingarn Medal, 1961; fellow, American Psychological Association; Phi Beta Kappa; Sigma Xi; author, *Desegregation: An Appraisal of the Evidence*, 1953; *Prejudice and Your Child*, 1955; *Dark Ghetto*, 1965; *Argument*, 1969. (See also *Current Biography: September 1964*.)

CONNOR, JOHN T. (1914-   ). Born, Syracuse, New York; A.B., magna cum laude, Syracuse University, 1936; LL.B., Harvard University, 1939; admitted to New York bar, 1939; practiced with firm of Cravath, de Gersdorff, Swain & Moore, 1939-42; general counsel, Office of Scientific Research and Development, Washington, D.C.

1942-44; vice president, Merck & Company, 1950-55; president and director, 1955-65; director of several corporations; trustee, Manhattanville College of the Sacred Heart; Syracuse University; USMC, 1944-45; counsel, Office of Naval Research and special assistant to the Secretary of the Navy, 1945-47; United States Secretary of Commerce, 1965-67; president, Allied Chemical Corporation, 1967- ; chairman and executive officer, 1969- ; member, Business Council; Council on Foreign Relations; Phi Beta Kappa; recipient, Presidential Certificate of Merit. (See also *Current Biography: April 1961*.)

DUBOS, RENÉ JULES (1901-). Born, Saint Brice, France; graduate, Collège Chaptal, Paris, 1919; B.S., Institut National Agronomique, Paris, 1921; Ph.D., Rutgers University, 1927; Sc.D., Rutgers University, 1927; University of Rochester, 1941; Harvard University, 1942; University of Paris, 1950; in United States, 1924- ; naturalized citizen, 1938; in French army, 1921-22; instructor of bacteriology, Rutgers University, 1924-27; Rockefeller Institute of Medical Research, 1927- ; professor, Rockefeller University, 1957- ; professor, Harvard Medical School, 1942-44; recipient, John Phillips Memorial Award, 1940; Howard Taylor Ricketts Award, University of Chicago, 1958; Scientific Achievement Award, American Medical Association, 1964; Pulitzer Prize for *So Human an Animal*, 1969; author, *The Bacterial Cell*, 1945; *Bacterial and Mycotic Infections of Man*, 1948; *Louis Pasteur—Free Lance of Science*, 1950; *Mirage of Health*, 1959; *The Dreams of Reason*, 1961; *The Touch of Life*, 1962; *Reason Awake*, 1970, and others; discoverer of tyrothricin. (See also *Current Biography: October 1952*.)

HUNT, EVERETT LEE (1890-). Born, Colfax, Iowa; A.B., Huron College, 1913; A.M., University of Chicago, 1921; Litt.D., Huron College, 1938; instructor, debate and oratory, Huron College, 1913-18; assistant professor of public speaking, Cornell University, 1918-25; professor of public speaking, Swarthmore College, 1925; professor of English and dean of men, Swarthmore College, 1934-58; since retirement, visiting professor of rhetoric, Cornell University, University of Hawaii, and Colorado State University; co-editor (with A. M. Drummond), *Persistent Questions in Public Discussion*, 1924; editor, *Quarterly Journal of Speech*, 1927-30; recipient John Nason Award for Distinguished Service to Swarthmore College, 1958; author, *The Revolt of the College Intellectual,* 1963; many essays and reviews.

MUSKIE, EDMUND SIXTUS (1914-). Born, Rumford, Maine; A.B., Bates College, 1936; LL.B., Cornell University, 1939; LL.D., Bates College; University of Maine; Bowdoin College, College of William and Mary, and others; admitted to Massachusetts bar, 1939; Maine bar, 1940; practiced law, Waterville, Maine, 1940, 1945-51; member, Maine House of Representatives, 1947-51, 1952-55; governor of Maine, 1955-59; United States Senate (Democrat, Maine) 1959- ; candidate for Vice President, 1968; member, National Democratic Committee, 1952-55; trustee, Bates College; member, Cornell University Law School Council; USNR, 1942-45; Phi Beta Kappa; Delta Sigma Rho; member, United States Senate Committee on Banking and Currency; Committee on Government Operations; Committee on Public Works; chairman, Subcommittee on Air and Water Pollution. (See also *Current Biography: December 1968.*)

McGILL, WILLIAM JAMES (1922-). Born, New York City; A.B., Fordham University, 1943; A.M., 1947; Ph.D., Harvard University, 1953; teaching fellow, Harvard University, 1948-49; staff member, Massachusetts Institute of Technology, 1951-54; assistant professor of psychology, Columbia University, 1956-58; associate professor, 1958-60; professor, 1960-65; chairman, psychology department, 1961-63; professor of sociology, University of California, San Diego, 1965-68; chancellor, 1968-70; president, Columbia University September 1, 1970- ; Phi Beta Kappa; Sigma Xi; member, American Statistical Association; Biometric Society; Psychometric Society; American Association for the Advancement of Science; Society of Experimental Psychologists.

NIXON, RICHARD M. (1913-). Born, Yorba Linda, California; A.B., Whittier College, 1934; LL.B., Duke University, 1937; law, Whittier, California, 1937-41; attorney with Office of Emergency Management, Washington, D.C., 1942; lieutenant commander, USN, 1942-46; United States House of Representatives (Republican, California), 1947-51; United States Senate, 1951-53; elected Vice President of the United States, 1952; reelected, 1956; Republican candidate for President, 1960; resumed law practice, Los Angeles, 1961, New York, 1963-68; elected President of the United States, 1968; author, *Six Crises,* 1962. (See also *Current Biography: June 1958.*)

SARA, MARTHA J. (1945-   ). Born, Bethel, Alaska; graduate, Bethel high school, 1963; A.A. in nursing, East Los Angeles College, 1965; R.N., 1965; associated with Public Health Service Hospital, Bethel Prenatal Home, 1966-67; Social Services Department, Bureau of Indian Affairs, 1967-69; student, University of Alaska, 1969-   ; University of Alaska delegate to Washington Summer Intern Program, Washington, D.C., 1970-   ; staff assistant, Medical-Surgical Research Department, Veterans Administration, summer 1970.

SEABORG, GLENN T. (1912-   ). Born, Ishpeming, Michigan; A.B., University of California at Los Angeles, 1934; Ph.D., University of California, at Berkeley, 1937; instructor in chemistry, University of California, at Berkeley, 1939-41; assistant professor, 1941; professor, 1945; announced discovery of plutonium (atomic number 94), 1940; associated with Manhattan Project on creation of atomic bomb, 1942-46; returned to teaching, 1946; associate director, Lawrence Radiation Laboratory, 1954-58; member of advisory committee to Atomic Energy Commission, 1946-50; shared Nobel Prize in chemistry with E. M. McMillan for work on transuranium elements, 1951; recipient, Fermi Award, 1959; member of President Eisenhower's science advisory committee, 1959; chancellor, University of California at Berkeley, 1958-61; chairman, Atomic Energy Commission, 1961-   ; contributor to scientific journals; co-author, *Comprehensive Inorganic Chemistry I,* 1953; *The Chemistry of the Actinide Elements,* 1957; *Elements of the Universe,* 1958. (See also *Current Biography: December 1961.*)

SMITH, MARGARET CHASE (1897-   ). Born, Skowhegan, Maine; graduate, Skowhegan high school, 1916; teacher, Skowhegan schools, 1916; honorary degrees from many institutions, including Bowdoin College, University of North Carolina, Temple University, Columbia University, and University of New Brunswick; executive officer, *Independent Reporter,* for eight years; treasurer, New England Waste Process Company, 1928; served on Republican State Committee of Maine, 1930-36; past president, Maine Federation of Business and Professional Women's Clubs; United States House of Representatives (Republican, Maine), 1940-48; United States Senate, 1949- ; member, Senate Committee on Appropriations; Committee on Armed Services; Committee on Aeronautical and Space Sciences. (See also *Current Biography: March 1962*.)

STANTON, FRANK (1908-). Born, Muskegon, Michigan; A.B., Ohio Wesleyan University, 1930; A.M., Ohio State University, 1932; Ph.D., 1935; LL.D., Ohio Wesleyan University, 1946; Birmingham Southern College, 1946; instructor in psychology, Ohio State University, 1932-35; joined Columbia Broadcasting System in 1935; research staff, 1935-38; director of research, 1938-42; vice president and general executive, 1942-46; vice president and general manager, 1945-46; president, 1946- ; associate director, Office of Radio Research, Princeton University, 1937-40; chairman, United States Advisory Commission on Information; trustee and former chairman, Center for Advanced Study in the Behavioral Sciences; trustee, Rand Corporation; member, Business Council; trustee, the Rockefeller Foundation; Carnegie Institution of Washington; director, Lincoln Center for the Performing Arts; fellow, American Academy of Arts and Sciences; American Association for the Advancement of Science; American Psychological Association; recipient, 1962 gold medal of the Radio and Television Executives Society; George Foster Peabody Award, 1961; Michael Friedsam Medal, 1964; special citation, American Institute of Architects, 1967; Advertising Council's Public Service Award, 1969; honorary president, Sigma Delta Chi, 1968; coauthor, *Students' Guide—The Study of Psychology*, 1935; film editor, *Some Psychological Reactions to Emotional Stimuli*, 1932; coeditor, *Radio Research*, 1941, 1942-43. (See also *Current Biography: October 1965*.)

CUMULATIVE AUTHOR INDEX

1960-1961—1969-1970

A cumulative author index to the volumes of REPRESENTATIVE AMERICAN SPEECHES for the years 1937-1938 through 1959-1960 appears in the 1959-1960 volume.